Birthing a Greater Reality

A Guide for Conscious Evolution

Robert Brumet

ALSO BY THE AUTHOR

Finding Yourself in Transition
The Quest for Wholeness

Birthing a Greater Reality

A Guide for Conscious Evolution

Robert Brumet

Unity Village, MO 64065-0001

Birthing a Greater Reality
First Edition 2010

Unity Books titles are available at special discounts for bulk purchases for study groups, book clubs, sales promotions, book signings or fundraising. To place an order, call the Unity Customer Care Department at 1-866-236-3571 or email *wholesaleaccts@unityonline.org.*

Bible quotations are from the New Revised Standard version unless otherwise noted.

Cover design: Jenny Hahn, cover painting *Innerverse* ©2010 Jenny Hahn. *www.jenspaintings.com*

Interior design: The Covington Group, Kansas City, Missouri

Library of Congress Control Number: 2010933801
ISBN: 978-0-87159-347-4
Canada BN 13252 0933 RT

To my dear friend,
Nancy Hiscoe Clark:

Wherever you may be
in
God's Grand Universe

ACKNOWLEDGEMENTS

I am indebted to my many teachers who have—directly or indirectly—been influential in the creation of this book. I honor each of them: Ken Wilber, Hameed Ali, Rodney Smith, Jack Kornfield, Andrew Cohen and many others too numerous to name.

I deeply appreciate the love and support I have received from friends and family members who have given me guidance and encouragement during the long process of writing this book. I particularly want to thank Shellie Bassett, Michael Maday and Leonard Scotto for their diligent research and constructive feedback, all of which was essential for this work to be what it is.

CONTENTS

PROLOGUE

I've known Robert coming on 20 years. He first became my tennis partner, then my friend. Soon he was to become my author as I worked with him through his first two books, *Finding Yourself in Transition* and *The Quest for Wholeness*, as his editor. Now I have found myself doing that again with this work.

I've also gotten to know Robert as a masterful teacher, having volunteered to sit in on many of his classes over at Unity Institute. I enjoyed how skillfully he would introduce and explore psychological themes along with the pastoral principles he was charged to teach. I give him full credit for raising the psychological awareness of an entire generation of Unity ministers! I saw him present integral philosopher Ken Wilber's *No Boundary*, a book and a class that challenged everyone, and certainly pushed the envelope of Unity's teachings. It was exciting to be part of it, and I have even been privileged to substitute teach for him on more than a few occasions.

In essence, what Wilber says is that there is a spectrum of consciousness that can be seen as a kind of map, and that like any good map, it can be used to help us locate where we are, and help us find where we are going. Practical as that sounds, it is also brilliant because it carefully addresses those perennial philosophical questions: Who am I? Where am I going? These basic questions are so often overlooked in our spiritual teachings because we often assume we already know the answers. "I" am my ego/personality. Where I am going is usually answered by my religion.

The traditional goal is to be going to heaven, thank you very much.

In Unity and New Thought circles, as well as in many others these days, "heaven" has ceased to be a location after death, but rather a state of mind here and now. In a real sense, our goal then has become to create heaven here on Earth, and a number of techniques are taught to accomplish that, including positive thinking, intentionality, affirmations and visualizations. Self-improvement and self-growth have become ends unto themselves. All this is fine, of course, but the journey seems endless, like we are the Israelites who fled Egypt in pursuit of the Promised Land only to find ourselves in a desert wilderness. Aside from mirages that disappear as we enter them, there is no end in sight. In this wilderness, the perennial question re-emerges: I am getting healthier, I am growing, yes, but still *where am I going?*

Robert and I have often discussed the idea that spiritual teachings, including those of Unity and New Thought, are usually presented within a "flatland" perspective. This term is borrowed from the E. A. Abbot novel *Flatland,* in which a two-dimensional world is visited by a third dimensional being. In a world of only length and width, no one can imagine, let alone see "depth." Yet depth is real. Similarly when we only perceive our growth in a horizontal plane, without a vertical axis, we are severely limited in our perceptions. What is desperately needed is a vertical shift to our understanding.

Through Brumet's earlier works, and through his teachings, he has addressed this need. In *Finding Yourself in Transition* he spoke to the evolutionary "cry" that calls us to go beyond our limits despite the very human desire to build fences and keep ourselves safe and secure. In *The Quest for Wholeness,* he introduced many ideas from Jungian and transpersonal psychology to help us understand that there is more to us than just our personality and ego, and the divinity we tend to call "the Christ" or "the God

Self." He spoke to the dark side of our lives and the need for us to integrate it. Without traveling through our darkness, feeling it, and releasing it, we cannot receive its power into our psyche. Without it, we cannot know our wholeness, and without that, our divinity.

Now in this new book, Brumet has more fully developed his map of consciousness, revealing to us the depth as well as the length and width of our journey. He speaks much more to the evolutionary cry that has most of us under its spell, whether we call it that or even think of it in those terms. The importance of this map can hardly be exaggerated.

Life is confusing. This brings to mind the ancient Chinese curse of "May you live in interesting times!" A while ago the United States of America elected its first African-American president under a wave of optimism and hope that had to be experienced to be believed. It was a call for change, and many could feel its evolutionary underpinning. Yet what happened next is that this optimism and hope quickly changed to pessimism and disappointment. Without arguing the specific issues, what is going on?

In developmental terms, change takes place in two major ways: translation and transformation. The flatland perspective conflates the two, and treats them as just one force, the popular term "transformation." Once again, I will rely on Ken Wilber's understanding. Translation is what happens when we have a powerful experience and some penetrating insights but then essentially go back to living our lives the way we were. We say we are changed, but, in practice, we cling to our habitual comforts and adapt, and return to what we know. In true transformation, however, our lives are altered, like the butterfly out of the chrysalis, and we can no longer live as the caterpillar.

Translation has its role to play. It tests ego boundaries, and it challenges us to a degree, much like a good Sunday lesson can cause us to reflect on our lives. Yet true transformation causes the death of the ego, or of an aspect of ego, and is, I'm sure, what Paul had in mind when he spoke of following Jesus by "dying daily." What constitutes this "ego," this sense of self-identity, is who we think we are and it does not surrender easily, leaving a lot of what we call transformation, in reality, mere translation. When we do transform, we evolve, and we are dealing with a true alchemy, not merely shifting surfaces. We are becoming new people, not just changing our clothes.

None of this happens quickly. We have become so accustomed to change being instantaneous that when it takes its time, and is part of a larger process, we become confused and disoriented. We need a larger view, a bigger map, as well as patience and persever-ance. The issues that confound us and touch our deepest feelings, including our anger and fear, are actually part of the developmen-tal process.

I'm reminded here of Teilhard de Chardin's description of how new species are born in nature. Pressure builds up in a *phylum*—a life system—until a point is reached where a new *peduncle*—a new life form—bursts forth as a new bud of a whole new phylum; or the pressure subsides and the system regresses back into itself, sta-bilizes, and remains the same, at least for the moment. Yet the urge to grow, to create, to move upwards in evolution, will eventually cause the system to try again at a later point.

The pressure is on, and we all feel it. Robert Brumet's book is superbly timed to give us the necessary perspective to see our challenge and our opportunity. The change we can believe in is our own evolutionary journey. Pregnancy is rarely easy, and yet, here we are about to give birth to a greater reality.

Michael Maday

Michael A. Maday is an ordained Unity minister, adjunct faculty at Unity Institute and Seminary, and former editor of Unity Books. Michael has a master's in transformational psychology.

INTRODUCTION

About 100,000 years ago a gradual, but very powerful, shift was occurring on our planet. For the first time since the origin of life on earth more than 3.5 billion years ago, the leading edge of evolution shifted from biological evolution to the evolution of consciousness. Since that time we have changed very little physically, but look how far, and how fast, we have come in just 100,000 years. (This is a long time for us, but it's only three-thousandths of one percent of the history of life on earth.) Evolution has shifted into high gear![1]

About 200 years ago another profound shift occurred. At that time a few individuals began to see that we are now responsible for our own evolution. We are becoming *evolution itself.* As we personally evolve in consciousness, we are advancing the evolution of all life on earth!

Right now we are at another critical point in human history and in the evolution of consciousness; the choices that we make in the near future are crucial. This is so not only because of the mind-rattling events and changes that have occurred in recent decades—along with the unprecedented dangers precipitated by some of them—but also because it seems that, like never before, the time is ripe for a quantum leap in conscious evolution.

We are living in a new era, an era not defined by the calendar or even by world events, but by an incipient transformation of consciousness that now rests upon the horizon of our vision.

Many are aware of this, but cannot name it. Such awareness can cause excitement, anticipation, anxiety or dread, depending on the readiness of the psyche to acknowledge it. For many, this awareness is a clarion call to awakening. For some, it is a call to action.

The most important choice facing us today is the willingness to do the work of transforming consciousness—beginning with ourselves. This last phrase marks the most difficult part. Many may be ready for someone else's consciousness to be transformed, and we may have been waiting for a long time! But it just doesn't seem to work that way. We can begin only with ourselves.

We begin this work by recognizing the illusions that keep us asleep and addicted to conflict and suffering. Indeed, conflict and suffering are symptoms of our illusions. Just as we check for fever to see if the body is ill, we look at the rough edges of our life to discover our illusions.

To be transformed we must be willing to do the vital work of personal healing and awakening—both within ourselves and within our personal relationships. Suffering is often catalyzed by others. By their presence or by their absence, they rub against the raw spots of our psyche, making us aware of our need for healing. Focusing on the faults of another is a common way of avoiding a look at our own unhealed wounds. Our personal healing depends upon this willingness to look at and compassionately accept what is there.

As we do this transformative work, both personally and interpersonally, we set the stage for global transformation—even if we aren't trying to do so. A fascinating, and perhaps inexplicable, relationship exists between personal and global transformation; perhaps they are two sides of the same coin. As soon as we begin the work of personal transformation, we are already engaging in global transformation. We are all related in profound and mysterious ways.

We use birthing as a metaphor for this process of transformation because it parallels that process in so many ways. A natural process, birthing cannot be controlled or dictated by human will; it has a life cycle and timetable of its own. Yet it requires human preparation and cooperation or else great suffering can result. Birthing is almost always painful, but our degree of understanding and our cooperation with this process can minimize that pain. Birthing is typically a joyous process; it normally results in a brand-new life—a life that is not ours, yet is very much a part of ourselves. And, there is always the possible misfortune of miscarriage or stillbirth; not all transformations are successfully completed.

All the same, evolution is on our side; it is the river in which our lives flow. The river moves us whether we like it or not, but we can no longer drift mindlessly. We are at the point where we must evolve consciously. Yes, we still go with the flow, but we now influence the course of that flow.

Evolution no longer occurs entirely unconscious of itself. We must now understand this process—and even more, we must *become* the process. It is time for us to become conscious evolutionaries and bring forth the needed global transformation. We are pioneers blazing the trail that will be followed by generations to come.

This book has three general parts. Chapters 1 and 2 focus on the big picture of who we are and of our history. We start from the very beginning of time and come up to the present moment as we look at who we are, why we are here, and what choices lie before us at this point in our evolutionary journey. We look at a few frameworks for evolutionary theory in order to determine both the direction and the crucial factors embedded in the evolutionary process.

Chapters 3, 4 and 5 parallel this approach, but here we focus on the personal level. Who am I, and why am I here? We unconsciously develop answers to those questions before we are aware of asking them. To transform, we must explore these answers and reconsider them at the deepest level of our identity.

Chapter 6 is where we integrate our understanding of global evolution with the wisdom derived from personal transformation. We then have a blueprint for that which is ours to do. As we align our heart's deepest desire with the direction of evolution, we become God's hands and feet in this evolving universe of form.

1

A Brief History of You

Before the beginning of time, the One rested in Omnipotence, for there was nothing impossible for Her. Then She rested in Omnipresence, for She had no limitations whatever. She began to rest in Omniscience; for it seemed there was nothing She did not know ... but the One developed a strange uneasiness: "If there is nothing I cannot do, then I cannot know what it means to be powerless. If I have no limitations, then I cannot know what it means to be limited. Therefore, there is something that I do not know! How can I be omniscient?

"How can I truly know power," She pondered, "if I cannot experience powerlessness? How can I truly know limitlessness, if I have never experienced limitation? How can I understand darkness, if I am nothing but light? How can I know anything, if I have never experienced its opposite?" These questions haunted Her for a long time, or would have if time had been invented yet!

But the One, being truly omniscient, found a solution to this dilemma: "There *is* a way I can experience opposites simultaneously. I *can* be Omnipresent and limited at the same time. I *can* be Omnipotent and powerless at the same time. Only then will I truly know power and love and light!

"I will dream that I am powerless. I will dream that I am limited. In my dream, I will experience all kinds of pain and limitation. As I awaken, the memory of this dream will teach me the ultimate nature of love and power and wisdom. For without illusion, I cannot fully understand the nature of reality."

And so the One said, "Let there be Light ... and there was a Big Bang ... and there was time and space and matter ... and the dream began.

Now it was no small feat to create this universe. It had to be ordered and balanced with incredible precision. For instance, if the energy of the Big Bang had been too strong, matter would have scattered too far apart and the universe would have eventually disintegrated; but if that same energy had been too weak, the universe would have soon collapsed upon itself. If electromagnetic forces were too strong, then stars would collapse upon themselves before matter could evolve far enough to support life; but if electromagnetic forces were too weak, these same stars would be incapable of having planets. If the universal strong force was too weak, no complex organic molecules could form and thus physical life would not be possible; but if that strong force were too strong, then nothing beyond helium would have formed and life would not be possible. And ... well, you get the picture ... let's just say that it wasn't easy!

The Story of You

The Big Bang occurred nearly 14 billion years ago. And about 10 billion years after this Big Bang, you—the living soul of humanity—were born into physical form.

You were born on a small planet circling a fairly average star located somewhere near the edge of a spiral galaxy. There were more than 100 billion such stars in this galaxy and over 100 billion such galaxies in the universe at that time. This planet, now named

Earth, formed more than 4 billion years ago; but it was less than a billion years old upon your arrival.

Your beginnings were indeed humble: A few protein molecules decided to get together and to make something of themselves ... and voilà, you were born! For more than 2 billion years you were just a single-celled creature. But then you discovered sex and things really took off! Just a billion years later you developed a backbone, and only 300 million years after that you were feeding milk to your babies.

About 2 million years ago you found yourself in your present form: a hairless primate that learned to walk upright. You learned to use tools, and eventually, speech. About 200,000 years ago you became Homo sapiens: *wise man*. Then in the blink of a cosmic eye, you were walking on the moon! You have learned language and music and science and poetry and many wonderful things; but more important, you are beginning to discover *yourself*.

About 100,000 years ago you became Homo sapiens sapiens; not just *wise* man, but *wise, wise* man. You began to understand that you understand. You became aware that you were aware. You began to discover your own wisdom and power and beauty. And now you are starting to discover what you *really* are. You are beginning to awaken from the dream.

Your long birth has been chronicled in many of your myths and legends. One that may be familiar to you is the one where you were named Adam, and you lived in a paradisiacal reality with your partner Eve. According to this story, you were expelled from this paradise for disobedience—and so it seems that you did disobey the Lord. But there is another, more important reason why you needed to leave: You grew up.

Your disobedience was not a sign of moral ineptitude, but rather a sign that you were no longer a creature—you were ready to become a co-creator. One might say that you *graduated* from the Garden of Eden. And upon graduation, it was time to find a job.

And so you began to "toil all the days of your life" and to "earn your bread by the sweat of your brow" (Gen. 3:18-19). The early days of co-creation were not that easy!

Your partner Eve ate of the fruit of the Tree of the Knowledge of Good and Evil, not only because it was "good for food, and that it was a delight to the eyes," but also because the fruit was "to be desired to make one wise" (Gen. 3:6). And when you ate of it "the eyes of both of them were opened" (Gen. 3:7). And the Lord said, "See, the man has become like one of us, knowing good and evil" (Gen. 3:22).

You then discovered the purpose of your creation in flesh: to know both good and evil, right and wrong, pleasure and pain. By experiencing the polarities of life in this dream-universe, you began to discover why you are here: to be the eyes and the ears, the hands and the feet of the One.

As the eyes and ears of the One, you are destined to awaken within the dream. You are destined to know yourself as a limited, temporal human being living in a physical universe, and simultaneously, to know yourself as unlimited, existing beyond time and space, ever-present and eternal. As the hands and feet of the One, you are destined to be a co-creator of the universe—this universe of time, space and form.

You, in essence, are the One dreaming that she is you as an individualized personality. And by remembering who you truly are in the midst of the polarities and limitations of this dream-world, you are fulfilling the purpose of your life on this planet.

Angels in Disguise

About 500 years ago a young Italian named Giovanni Pico della Mirandola delivered a brilliant oration to a convention of scholars wherein he spoke as The One spoke to Adam at the time of his creation:

Neither an established place, nor a form belonging to you alone, nor any special function have We given to you, O Adam, and for this reason, that you may have and possess, according to your desire and judgment, whatever place, whatever form, and whatever functions you shall desire. The nature of other creatures, which has been determined, is confined within the bounds prescribed by Us. You, who are confined by no limits, shall determine for yourself your own nature, in accordance with your own free will, in whose hand I have placed you. I have set you at the center of the world, so that from there you may more easily survey whatever is in the world. We have made you neither earthly nor heavenly, neither mortal nor immortal, so that, more freely and more honorably the molder and maker of yourself, you may fashion yourself in whatever form you shall prefer. You shall be able to descend among the lower forms of being, which are brute beasts; you shall be able to be reborn out of the judgment of your own soul into the higher beings, which are divine.[1]

According to most theories of evolution, we *have* chosen to descend among the lower forms of being, to become the brute beast, and then to be reborn into a higher form of being. The theme of evolution may be seen as that of continuous birthing into a greater reality.

At this point in our evolution, we humans find ourselves "halfway between the beasts and the angels," disguised as Homo sapiens sapiens. We have exhibited both the best and the worst of each, as human history has shown us. We have soared much higher than the angels, and we have behaved much lower than the beasts.

Humans have climbed to magnificent heights in many arenas. The past century has seen achievements that would be totally unimaginable in the century preceding it. Through genetic engineering we can replicate and control life forms; with artificial intelligence we have created devices that surpass human thinking capabilities; through organ transplants and other miracles of medical science we can prolong human life by many years. In 1903 the first airplane soared to an altitude of 10 feet. Just 66 years later we landed on the moon: altitude 238,857 miles.

In the social arena we have made breakthroughs never before possible: In the United States, 150 years after African slaves were owned as property and treated like farm animals, a man of African descent is elected as president. He was competing for the position with a woman, whom nine decades earlier would not have been permitted to vote in a presidential election.

We have soared to great heights. But in many ways we have descended much lower than the beasts. In the past century more than 100 million people have been killed by war and genocide. (This is equal to the population of the entire planet at the time of Socrates.) In the last decade of this same century, over 100 million children have died from starvation or malnutrition. Those deaths could have been prevented for what the world's nations spend on their military every 48 hours.

The Crisis Point

At the start of the 21st century, we find ourselves at a crucial juncture in this human experience. Having acquired powers undreamed of by our ancestors, we seem in many ways godlike. But we have not evolved the wisdom needed to broker these powers. In this regard we have become more like the beasts than the angels. This is a very dangerous circumstance; we are like a small child with a loaded gun.

For the first 99.99 percent of humanity's time on earth, the greatest threat to existence came from the vagaries of nature: wild animals, microbes, parasites, climactic changes and natural disasters. But today the greatest threat to human existence is humanity itself. Of the many possible scenarios for our collective demise, most are the result of human behavior. If the human species were to become extinct, the most likely culprit would be ourselves. We have met humanity's greatest enemy—and they are us. This statement is true for no species other than ours. It is the greatest of paradoxes that the presumably most intelligent species on this planet is also the most self-destructive.

Our development has become dangerously one-sided. We have achieved an astounding degree of knowledge of the material world, and we remain appallingly ignorant of ourselves. We have overdeveloped knowledge and underdeveloped wisdom. This lopsided development has forced us into a position where we must become more balanced or we may perish as a species.

The answer does not lie in negating the progress we have achieved and returning to some idealized primitive past. The problem lies not in knowledge, or technology, or in the material world itself. The problem lies in the tremendous imbalance and the lack of integration between our inner and our outer worlds. We have failed to parallel our rampant external development with a corresponding growth in self-awareness. We have created external wealth and internal poverty.

Because of this internal poverty, we have developed a culture that attempts to fill its inner emptiness with material possessions, with pleasure, with entertainment and social status. We have developed a lifestyle that uses both people and Earth's resources to fill our inner emptiness. We have become a highly addictive culture. This has led to rampant consumerism and to near depletion of many of our planets resources.

Paralleling our lagging wisdom is our lagging compassion. Our blindness to the deeper aspects of ourselves is reflected in our blindness to much of humanity. The state of humankind is always a reflection of the collective human psyche. This blindness has lead to huge disparities in the distribution of wealth, education, power and privilege: The richest 1 percent of the world's population owns 40 percent of the world's wealth; while the poorest half of the world's population—about 3.5 billion human beings—owns barely 1 percent of the world's wealth.

In many ways it would seem that the dream of the One has become a nightmare. And what is the solution to a nightmare? We may wish to change the bad dream into a happy one, but a more direct and permanent solution is to simply wake up. Yet something is keeping us asleep. What is it that keeps us in this slumber? Discovering the answer to this question can help us to awaken.

In the biblical story of creation, Adam falls into a deep slumber. Nowhere in this story, nor anywhere else in the Bible, does it say that Adam awakened. It is not mentioned because it has not happened. Adam remains asleep.

Adam's slumber is the major cause of our crisis. The crisis before us is not a political or economic or even psychological crisis, it is a spiritual crisis. The vast majority of us do not know who or what we truly are, and this ignorance may destroy us. Waking up has become an evolutionary necessity. It is no longer optional. So let's look at what keeps us asleep.

Survival of the Fittest

Every biological species has evolved a certain strategy for survival. Some animals have claws, sharp teeth, hard shells, horns, fur, camouflage, and so on, as survival weapons and tools. For many species, certain instinctive behaviors are strategies for survival; hunting, foraging, migrating, hibernating, burrowing or climbing trees are examples.

When we look at the human body, we see very little that would insure our survival in the wild. Our body lacks claws, fur or protective armor; almost any animal can outrun us, and we have relatively few survival instincts. Without restaurants and grocery stores, most of us would starve to death! Completely helpless at birth, we remain in need of parental protection and care for many years; much longer than any other species. Amazingly, ours is the dominant species on this planet!

We are the dominant species for one reason alone: Rather than adapting to the natural world solely through biological evolution, we have evolved a brain that gives us the ability to create internal representations of the outer world. We are able to create an internal virtual world. And we have developed the ability to manipulate our inner worlds in very creative ways.

We are able to create a hypothetical reality: a "what if" world. We have learned to become like gods in this hypothetical inner world. In our minds we can take things apart and put them back together in some very ingenious ways. We have learned to reproduce our internal creations externally. We can manipulate our world in ways unavailable to other species because we have an internal universe wherein we have become a god. And we are then able to fashion our outer world to replicate our inner world. Rather than evolving claws and sharp teeth, we have developed powerful weapons and tools. Instead of migrating south, or growing fur, we create warm clothing and comfortable heated dwellings.

Our internal virtual reality is more adaptable to change than any physical body. We can change our internal maps and strategies much more quickly than it takes an animal to evolve biological changes. When environmental conditions change, we can readily adapt our tools and dwellings and clothing to the new environment, as opposed to going extinct or spending 50 million years evolving a new physical form. (What a drag that would be!)

With this brain and its ability to create virtual realities, we have developed speech and written communication that allow us to pass these survival strategies on to subsequent generations much faster than is possible via biological evolution. We have created cultures, wherein vital knowledge is passed on to later generations, who may then improve upon these strategies. As individuals, we both inherit and influence our cultural knowledge. Perhaps we may play a part in its evolution.

So What Is the Problem?

Nothing I've said so far sounds like bad news—and it isn't. Our survival strategy is actually an evolutionary stroke of genius. The problem is that the human mind, an evolutionary tool designed to help us survive, is no longer our servant; *it has become our master.*

We have become identified with this mind; we think it is who we really are. Thus, we have not recognized its limitations, and we are attempting to use this wonderful tool for purposes beyond which it has evolved.

The One is awakening within the world of form. She is gradually awakening from the dream. But the primary tool that we have evolved in order to physically survive is being used to keep us asleep. Human thought has done an amazing job of helping us to survive, but it cannot wake us up. It cannot go beyond itself.

Yet we don't know what else to use, and we are afraid to abandon it because it has been our lifeline for hundreds of millennia. Evolution is calling us to awaken to a greater reality, but our mistaken attachment to our familiar survival tool is inhibiting that awakening.

We have said earlier that the crisis before us is a spiritual crisis: The vast majority of human beings do not know who or what we truly are. And this ignorance may destroy us. Let's explore this further.

Imagine that you are sitting at home when an uninvited stranger walks into the room. You inquire, "Excuse me, sir, but who are you?" He replies, "I don't know." Puzzled, you ask, "Where are you going?" "I don't know." "Well, where did you come from?" "I don't know." At this point you might consider calling the police or an ambulance because obviously this man needs help.

This fictional man is a symbol for virtually every one of us. If every human being on Earth were asked these questions, most of us would—if we were deeply honest—answer exactly the same way. But, paradoxically, this man is actually better off than most of us because he *knows* that he does not know who he is. Most of us don't know that. We already think that we know who we are.

We are like an Academy Award-winning actor who has developed a case of amnesia. We know our lines perfectly; we perform our role exquisitely. But we've forgotten who the actor is. What's more, we have forgotten that we have forgotten! We have become totally identified with our role and our script; we believe that it is reality.

In humanity's early days, we were identified with the body; but more recently, we have become identified primarily with the mind. Because we do not know who we are, we have identified with our survival strategies. If we were to let go of this habituated identification, we would feel like a turtle without its shell, or a tiger without its teeth or claws. Our primary survival tool would appear to vanish. This is frightening indeed.

The inclination to cling to an old strategy is a universal tendency. When animals (including humans) are frightened or traumatized, they typically will regress to an earlier form of behavior.

When afraid, we cling to that which gives us a sense of security. We typically revert to an old way of being in an attempt to feel safe rather than face the raw terror of the unknown.

This propensity exists within groups of people as well. When threatened, families, organizations and nations will hold onto what seems to be tried and true and will have little inclination to experiment with new ways of being. In times of crisis, patriotism, nationalism and the old-time values typically stage a comeback.

We may cling to these old ways even when common sense and personal experience tell us that it no longer works. That which we call dysfunctional behavior is the result of unconsciously clinging to an outmoded way of behaving and relating to others. Although this may cause great suffering in our life, we unwittingly cling to these old patterns because they are familiar and provide us with a sense of identity and security. To live without these internal maps to guide us, to interpret our reality and to make sense of our life experiences can be terrifying.

As a species, we have not yet discovered our true nature, and we thus have identified with our survival strategy. But our current survival strategy is not able to take us into the next phase of our evolution. We need to replace it with a greater reality. But we cling to that which is not working, thinking that it is what we are.

Giving up our strategies can feel like death itself, so we cling to the old identity. We are like the traveler who has driven beyond the territory defined by his map, yet he continues to use the obsolete map because it is the only one he has! We have believed our thoughts to be reality. We have mistaken our thoughts of who we are with the reality of who we are. We have the map confused with the territory.

Deep down, beneath our everyday awareness, we know that we don't know. There are two reasons most of us are unwilling to acknowledge this. First, facing this truth can result in considerable anxiety. Just ask most anyone to sit alone for one hour without thinking, talking, reading, watching TV or engaging in any of our usual self-distractions. For most people this would be quite difficult because a great deal of anxiety would arise. Why is this so? Because the anxiety is *already there*! When we stop distracting ourselves with physical and mental activity, it quickly arises into conscious awareness.

Second, we have a tacit collective agreement not to permit this anxiety to arise within us. In polite society we make sure that we do not have to come to grips with this. We have created a culture that contains innumerable distractions designed to avoid facing ourselves; it is designed to keep Adam asleep.

The Human Dilemma

Fortunately, something within us will not allow us to remain asleep for too long. As human beings, we have two very powerful internal forces pushing us in opposite directions. We have a survival instinct: the drive to survive in physical form. And this has been overlaid by the drive to survive as a psychological entity, as an individual ego. Sometimes this drive can be even stronger than the one for physical survival.

Yet within us is another very powerful drive: the divine impulse to grow, to evolve, and to become more than we seem to be. "Blowing through heaven and earth, and in our hearts and the heart of every living thing, is a gigantic breath—a great Cry—which we call God."[2] This drive for self-transcendence is present in all life forms, albeit unconscious in most of them. But, with some humans it has become conscious and may be very compelling.

This dilemma of self-preservation and self-transcendence is a central theme throughout human history. In nearly every human being, the tension of these conflicting forces is experienced to some degree, perhaps consciously, but most often not.

In Christian circles, we may hear someone observe that "Everyone wants to go to heaven, but no one wants to die to get there." In New Age circles this statement could be paraphrased as "Everyone wants spiritual transformation, but no one wants to sacrifice their ego-identity to attain it." To face the death of the body is not easy, but we all must, eventually. To face the death of the ego may be even more difficult, and relatively few of us do so.

Human beings will go to almost any length to preserve their identity. To lose it feels like death, or worse. Some human beings have also gone to incredible lengths to transcend their identity. The history of the human race is a fascinating drama depicting how we have played out these conflicting drives.[3]

This conflict is now being felt more poignantly than ever before. The tension between these two powerful forces is virtually palpable in our world today: caught between the beasts and the angels; torn between safety, comfort and security and the indomitable Cry within that demands that we come up higher. This tension is part of a crisis that is evoking us to birth a greater reality.

By deepening our understanding of both of these forces—the drive to maintain our present identity and the drive to evolve beyond it—we will be in a better position to facilitate this birth. The degree of conflict and suffering that we experience in this birthing process is a function of our understanding (or lack of it) and our willingness to consciously embrace this evolutionary transformation.

To the degree that we are unconscious, our evolution occurs with fits and starts, and with much conflict and suffering. We will evolve; that is a given. Whether that evolution occurs through a cataclysmic Armageddon experience or from a natural cosmic childbirth is largely up to us.

The First Steps

How to facilitate this birth is the subject of this book. I'll lay some groundwork. Later on we will explore the relevancy of the Buddhist philosophy and spiritual practice to our evolutionary journey. The heart of this philosophy is the Eight-fold Path of Awakening, which begins with two principles that are relevant to our present discussion. These principles are called Right Understanding and Right Motivation.

As facets of the awakening process, these principles are preceded by the word *right*, which might best be translated as "wise" or "skillful." In practice, these two are interrelated.

A brief focus on wise motivation is in order. Our very motivation to understand and to engage in the process of conscious evolution originates from within the evolutionary process itself. It is not something within us that is reaching for something outside of us; nor is it that something outside of us is influencing our inner motivation. This motivation to evolve is within us, and it surrounds us. It is the core of who we are.

We recognize that our motivation to evolve is itself part of the response. Our sense of wonder and of awe at the immense potential within us is itself a motivational force, and a response. Our desire to bring this potential into manifestation in our life and in the world is an expression of this evolutionary force.

As for wise understanding, the wonderful paradox is that both our desire to understand the evolutionary process and our motivation to engage it consciously are originating from within the evolutionary process itself. Evolution is requiring itself to become conscious. This reminds me of the well-known C. W. Escher drawing that portrays two hands: each one drawing the other! Our usual assumptions of cause and effect become baffled by this process. Cause and effect are reciprocal and indistinguishable.

Similarly, our familiar dichotomy of doing and not-doing is turned inside out. We are conditioned to think of ourselves as actively doing something from our own volition, or of passively doing nothing at all. Either we are responsible, or we are not; either we are in control, or we are not. We see our self as either active or at rest, giver or receiver, subject or object.

But the evolutionary impulse, the Cry, is done neither by us, nor for us, nor to us. It is done *through* us. We are instruments of it and for it. In this process, we are simultaneously active and passive, subject and object, seed and fruit. We are both alpha and omega. We are not a thing; we are a process. Not a noun but a verb.

The American philosopher John Boodin eloquently captures this sentiment. "We are part of a creative destiny, reaching backward and forward to infinity ... We are the fruition of a process that stretches back to star dust. We are material in the hands of the Genius of the universe for a still larger destiny that we cannot see ...."[4]

Evolution is natural: We cannot will it to occur or will it not to occur. However, conscious evolution requires our active consent and our active involvement. We cannot sleep through it. We must be willing to surrender to the divine will; otherwise it cannot unfold though us. Our primary work then is to see where we are unconsciously blocking the awareness and expression of the divine will. Likewise, conscious evolution may be considered a metaphor for the unfolding of the divine will—not to us or for us, but through us.

We unwittingly block the divine will—conscious evolution— not so much by what we don't know, but by what we know, but don't know that we know; in other words, by our unconscious beliefs and assumptions. We must know what we know and then discern if what we know is really true. If it isn't, then it must be released. And if we are not willing to release it, we need to see why we are holding on to it. Much of conscious evolution is simply becoming conscious of what we believe to be true.

Another paradox we encounter on our journey is that of what we call "personal" versus what we call "collective," or individual versus group, part versus whole. The transformation of consciousness must take place one person at a time. However, who we are as an individual—as a person—cannot be separated from our relationships and from our environment; who we are is always contextual. Human beings can never be considered solely as individuals because we are innately connected in a broader web.

This interconnectedness occurs in many ways and at many levels. Our personal reality is fundamentally embedded in a collective reality. Evolution and transformation can never be considered in isolation. To consider oneself as an individual and as part of a greater whole is to simply look at two facets of our being; they are intrinsically inseparable. We are like the electron that may behave like a wave or may behave like a particle, depending upon circumstances and perspective. We are both an individual and a collective. Personal transformation and global evolution are inseparable. We may consider each aspect separately. This may be helpful for our understanding, but in reality these are but two perspectives of our earthly expression.

Likewise our human nature is not apart from our divine nature; the absolute is not apart from the relative. Once again, these may be considered separately, but in reality they are simply different profiles of the same face. Evolution and transformation are different profiles of the same process separated only by the perspective of time. Both are descriptions of the One awakening from the great dream, the Grand Illusion.

In Summary

1. Each of us is the One dreaming that She is an individual personality. The purpose of life is to awaken from that dream; to know ourselves as limited human beings living in a physical universe, and simultaneously, to know our selves as unlimited and eternal.

2. The process of this awakening is called evolution. We now find ourselves at a crucial juncture in human history: We have attained godlike powers but have not developed the wisdom needed to broker these powers.

3. Our development has become dangerously one-sided. We have achieved an astounding degree of knowledge of the material world, yet we remain appallingly ignorant of ourselves. We have failed to parallel our external development with growth in self-awareness.

4. The crisis before us is a spiritual crisis: The vast majority of us do not know who or what we truly are. Waking up has become an evolutionary necessity; yet something is keeping us asleep.

5. Rather than adapting to the natural world through biological evolution, humans have evolved a brain that gives us the ability to create internal virtual worlds. We can change these internal maps more quickly than it takes to evolve biological changes. We have developed cultures that allow us to pass these survival strategies on to subsequent generations. When environmental conditions change, we can readily adapt.

6. The problem is that the human mind, designed to help us survive, is no longer our servant; it has become our master. We have become identified with this mind; we think it is who we really are. Thus, we are afraid to abandon it.

7. Evolution is calling us to awaken, but we have identified with our survival strategies and remain asleep. We have mistaken our thoughts of who we are with the reality of who we are. To let go of this identity is very frightening.

8. Humans have two very powerful internal forces pushing in opposite directions. We have the drive to maintain our existing identity and another drive to grow, to evolve, and to become more than we believe ourselves to be. The conflict between these two forces is being felt more poignantly now than ever before.

9. Two principles from the Buddhist tradition are relevant here: Right Understanding and Right Motivation. Paradoxically, both our desire to understand the evolutionary process and our motivation to engage it consciously are originating from within the evolutionary process itself. The evolutionary impulse occurs *through* us. Evolution is requiring itself to become conscious; it now requires our consent and active involvement.

10. Conscious evolution and personal transformation are different viewpoints of the same process. They are separated only from the perspective of time.

Segue

In any discussion of global transformation, an obvious question will arise: Where do we go from here? To address this question, we will take a long look backwards.

Global transformation has been in process since the beginning of time. We have called it evolution. To understand the direction we must move in, and the next step in our journey, we will explore some principles of this 13.7 billion-year-old transformational process called evolution.

2

Evolutionary Trail Markers

W e see an intricate relationship between personal transformation and global evolution. To be transformed personally and globally, we must align ourselves with the direction of evolution. But what is the direction of evolution? In this chapter we study the work of a number of scientists, philosophers and visionaries to discern where the "arrow of evolution" points.

Darwin v. God

When we hear the word *evolution* today, many of us think of Charles Darwin. Many people believe that Charles Darwin was the first to develop the concept of evolution; but this is far from true. Darwin developed a theory of natural selection, so-called "survival of the fittest," which he articulated in his book *On the Origin of Species by Means of Natural Selection*, published in 1859. Darwin was among the first to scientifically explore the principles of evolution. Today *evolution* is most commonly used to mean biological evolution, because this was the focus of Darwin's work. His work has been immensely important to our understanding of biological evolution, and it generated a public debate which rages on to this day.

Our news media revel in expounding issues of science versus religion. But the well-publicized debate of Darwinian evolution versus so-called Creation Science is really a bogus issue. There is no conflict between science and religion if we are true to the purpose of each of these disciplines.

Science uses empirical methods of observation and analysis to understand how the physical universe operates. Legitimate science does not address questions of ultimate meaning or questions regarding morality or values. Science addresses the question of how things work; it is not concerned with why things happen or what their ultimate purpose may be.

Religion *is* concerned with questions of ultimate meaning and value. Religion does not focus on how things physically work. Science is interested in how the natural world works, whereas religion legitimately asks questions regarding the value, meaning and purpose of the natural world.

Problems occur when either discipline tries to invade the domain of the other. When science is believed to be the sole legitimate method for answering *all* human questions, or when it attempts to answer questions of ultimate meaning or value, then science is being misused. This is called *scientism;* it is not legitimate science.

Conversely, some religious fundamentalists claim that religious dogma should override scientific knowledge regarding observable and verifiable facts within the natural world. This is a misuse of religion. The misuse of religion does not make religion itself invalid.

If someone believes that God created the universe and all in it and that there is an ultimate purpose for it, then that would comprise a legitimate religious belief. If someone (perhaps even the same person) believes that natural selection best explains how biological evolution works, then that is a legitimate scientific perspective. These views are not mutually exclusive. If someone uses religious doctrine to "prove" that the universe was created in seven days, then they are misusing religion.

Science and religion, or science and spirituality, can be legitimate partners in the search for truth because each has its own perspective and its own domain of inquiry. They can be great complements to one another, and have been used that way very effectively by many intelligent and deeply spiritual individuals.

The Evolution of Consciousness

Biologically, the human body has remained essentially unchanged for the past 50,000 years. Our brain still functions essentially the way it did when we were living on the African savannah. Our brain developed as it did in order for us to survive. Survival depended upon noticing small but sudden changes in our environment: a movement behind a bush; the snapping of a twig in the middle of the night; a pair of eyes appearing in the darkness. These changes signal danger, and the brain will instruct the body to respond accordingly.

Our brain was designed to detect immediate danger and to respond instantly: get ready for fight or flight. It was not designed to respond to very slow, subtle changes, or to long-term trends. Evolution did not teach us to respond to statistics. Our forbearers on the savannah were not concerned with overpopulation, climate change or resource depletion, as are we. But we are facing these dangers with the same brain that was designed to protect us from wild animals and spear-chucking enemies.

Dr. Robert Ornstein, a noted psychologist, writer, professor and chairman of the Institute for the Study of Human Knowledge, writes:

> Our biological evolution is for all practical purposes, at its end. There will be no further

> biological evolution without conscious evolu-
> tion. We have to take command of our evolution
> now and begin a massive program for conscious
> changes in the way we think … relate to others …
> identify with the rest of humanity.[5]

We are overdue for this "massive program" to which Ornstein refers. The future demise or transformation of humanity will not be the result of biological evolution, but will result from the evolution of consciousness. Therefore we will focus our attention primarily upon the evolution of consciousness, along with its promises and its challenges.

A Brief History of Evolution

The evolution of consciousness is not a new concept; it predates Darwin's work by many centuries. The earliest known written teachings on evolution are those of Anaximander, who lived in the sixth century BCE in Ionia, a Greek colony. About a hundred years later, the Greek philosopher Heraclitus developed many ideas that have inspired some modern philosophers in their theories of evolution.

In its modern form, the concept of evolution can be attributed to German philosopher and mathematician Gottfried Leibniz, who wrote *The Ultimate Origin of Things* in 1697. Another German philosopher, Georg Hegel, wrote *The Phenomenology of Spirit*, published in 1807, which revealed how history unfolds in a dialectical process wherein conflict makes possible the transformation to a higher state. This seminal work laid the foundation for the subsequent evolutionary understanding of the universe.[6] Other philosophers, scientists and visionaries that have since proposed theories of conscious evolution include Henri Bergson, Rudolf Steiner, Sri Aurobindo, Jean Gebser, Pierre Teilhard de Chardin,

Clare Graves, Alfred North Whitehead and Ken Wilber. We will explore ideas from many of these writers later in this chapter.

Pulled From Above

Darwin's theory of evolution focuses exclusively on biological evolution and generally assumes that evolution occurs from the bottom up; it assumes that evolution is pushed upward by nothing but restless dirt. We are being pushed from below by unknown forces, with an uncertain destination, guided only by environmental factors and by chance.

To effectively consider the evolution of consciousness, we must turn this idea on its head, and consider evolution as being "pulled from above." With this approach, evolution must be seen as having a purpose and that all of life and consciousness is being drawn into that purpose. Therefore, evolution is not just about the past; it is very much about the future as well.

Let us begin with the premise that evolution, including human history, has meaning because it is being drawn into something beyond itself. From this perspective, the purpose of evolution is for the Absolute to unfold itself within the relative universe. Likewise, human history is seen as the unfolding of the Absolute through the life and consciousness of humanity. Humanity discovers its deepest nature through the unfolding of its evolutionary history.[7]

This unfolding process occurs through human consciousness. The end of this process is to fulfill the ultimate potential of human consciousness: to consciously merge its identity with the Absolute; to recognize that humanity itself is a conscious expression of the Absolute, and that ultimately all that exists is an expression of the Absolute. This unfolding is in some ways determined and in some ways open-ended. The ultimate destination is determined; the path we take to arrive there is not. The path of unfolding follows specifically sequenced levels of consciousness.

The order of this sequence is fixed; how we move through them is not.

The description of these levels is part of an ancient Western wisdom tradition that depicts a hierarchical sequence of psychic structures called the Great Chain of Being. These levels are actually nested, one within the other, as concentric circles. The Great Chain of Being is a predetermined sequence of evolutionary levels: Matter to Body to Mind to Soul to Spirit. Evolution unfolds in this manner.

To fully understand evolution, we must understand the concept of involution. Involution occurs in the opposite direction of evolution. With involution Spirit *involves* itself in its creation. The created is infused with the Creator. They are not separate. Creation is simply a disguise for the Creator. The physical universe is but camouflage for the Absolute.

As in the opening story of this book, Spirit loses itself in this camouflage. It loses itself so that it can later find itself through the process of evolution—and perhaps discover new dimensions of its own being. This loss is entirely in appearance, not at all in reality—hence the "dreaming" referred to in the previous chapter. In reality, Spirit is everywhere fully present at all times—and even beyond time itself.

In the process of involution, Spirit "descends" down the Great Chain.[8] With each of these descents there is an experience of decreasing freedom and awareness, and an increasing sense of separation and objectification. With each descent, Spirit becomes identified with that corresponding level.

Spirit descends first into the level of soul. At this level, Spirit becomes individualized; it experiences a degree of limitation. It is no longer "all that is"; it is partial rather than complete. Existing beyond time and space as we know it, the soul's perspective transcends time, space and form, but it is not limitless.

As Spirit descends into the mind level, it becomes more limited in its functioning. The mind exists outside of space but inside of time. Time is a creation of the mind; it cannot comprehend timelessness. Time is the canvas upon which the mind paints its images. All thought is invested in the past or the future. To the mind there is no "now" because time appears as a river that is ceaselessly flowing. The mind is unable to grasp or to capture the river of time.

At the next descent, Spirit limits itself into to a physical body, a life form. The body is limited by both time and space; it can transcend neither. Whereas the mind cannot enter the now moment, the body cannot escape it; it knows nothing else. Sensation is the language of the body: pleasure, pain, heat and cold. Sensation occurs only in the present, never the past or future. Space is the medium of the body; it defines itself via space. Your body is spatial; it is here and not there.

Finally, Spirit descends into matter. Here it appears frozen, immobile and inert—the ultimate limitation. Matter is inert, but not dead. At this level, Spirit appears comatose, but it is still very much alive. It has life, but that life unfolds very slowly. The life of matter has its own timetable, which is measured in eons rather than months and years. Spirit is whole and complete within matter, as it is at every level. And, as such, matter contains the potential for all the levels above it, which unfold through evolution.

Evolution occurs in the reverse order: Spirit unfolds that which it enfolded in involution. Spirit "ascends" by awakening and transforming into the next level of the Great Chain. Through evolution, Spirit is slowly awakening to itself, beginning with the awakening of matter into living bodies.

Spirit evolves *through* matter, not from it. Matter is the vehicle for Spirit's awakening, not the source of it. Through evolution, Spirit "remembers" what was "lost" in involution. But to remember, Spirit must first *disidentify* itself from its identification with the existing level. Ken Wilber writes: "During involution each and every level is created not just by a forgetting of Spirit but as a substitute for Spirit. And therefore in evolution, as each level emerges, consciousness exclusively identifies with that substitute gratification until it has been thoroughly tasted and found wanting ... at that point the death of that level is accepted."[9]

Ironically, evolution involves a sequence of apparent deaths, one at each level of the Great Chain. But each death is followed by a rebirth into the next level. As matter awakens and evolves into a living body, there is a corresponding increase of freedom and awareness. Living beings (even single-celled creatures) have immensely more awareness and freedom than matter alone. This trend continues with the gradual evolution into ever more complex bodies and then to the level of mind. With the attributes of mind, which include thought and imagination, freedom and awareness are enormously increased. The mind can go where the body cannot. With the movement from mind to soul, we again experience a quantum leap into a new dimension of awareness and freedom—a level that is incomprehensible to the mind.

The final leap is that of ultimate transformation wherein matter, body, mind and soul experiences itself as being identical with Spirit. This is the goal of evolution; it is the direction toward which everything in the universe is moving. The prodigal son and the prodigal daughter will return to the Father after untold eons in the far country. And each return enriches the Father, which is the unchanging Spirit of infinite love and wisdom, patiently waiting for each of us to come home.

The French Connection

We continue our study of evolutionary maps with the work of Henri Bergson, who was born in Paris in 1859, the year of the publication of Charles Darwin's *On the Origin of Species*. Bergson was a university professor, specializing in Greek and

Latin philosophy. He created many significant philosophical works, and he won the Nobel Prize for literature in 1927. His most notable work was *Creative Evolution*, published in 1907, which constitutes one of the most profound and original contributions to the philosophical perspective of evolution.

Bergson argued that evolution is propelled by a force which imbues itself into organic matter. He referred to this force as the *élan vital* (vital impetus), which is none other than consciousness itself. The élan vital operates through evolution as a pressure, gradually forcing its way into ever higher levels of expression. The direction and purpose of evolution is to free consciousness from the constriction of matter.[10]

Pierre Teilhard de Chardin was deeply inspired by Bergson's work. Teilhard was born in Auvergne, France, in 1881. He was ordained a Jesuit priest in 1912, and was a stretcher-bearer in the First World War, for which he received several medals for bravery. Having received his doctorate in 1922, he eventually became a respected scholar in the field of geology and paleontology. He was deeply interested in the evolution of consciousness via his reading of Bergson.

His most significant work took place from 1923 through 1946, while he was in China. However Teilhard was forbidden by the Catholic Church to publish his remarkable works, so while he was alive, his most important writings remained unknown. Upon his death, his opus, *The Phenomenon of Man*, and other major works of his were published by a relative.

Teilhard believed that nature presents us with two faces. One is the exterior face of matter, which is of primary interest to the physical sciences; the other is the interior reality, or consciousness. He believed there to be a correspondence between these two, beginning with the most elemental particles and all the way up to humans. In the *Phenomenon of Man*, he writes: "Co-extensive with their Without, there is a Within of things."[11] The exterior world is inevitably aligned at every point with an interior one.

Teilhard believed that the evolution of complexity in the physical world is accompanied by evolution in the quality and the degree of consciousness in the interior world. He referred to this as the law of Complexity-Consciousness. This law operates in the opposite direction of the law of entropy, which points to the universe as moving slowly towards its inevitable death. When viewed solely from the exterior, it appears that the universe is winding down and slowly dying. When viewed from the interior aspect, the universe is not dying but clearly evolving toward some end.

Teilhard recognized two types of energy. One is tangential energy, the external component of energy, which links each element with others of the same order of complexity. The other type is radial energy, which is an internal energy, a psychic energy, which moves all things toward greater complexity and greater consciousness.

Tangential energy connects the exterior of things; radial energy connects the interior of things. He equated radial energy with love. He writes, "Love alone is capable of uniting living beings in such a way as to complete and fulfill them, for it alone takes them and joins them by what is deepest in themselves."[12]

The Omega Point

Biologists categorize various living species into groupings called *phyla*. If a particular phylum is depicted as a treelike structure in which individual species form the branches on this tree, then the stem of this treelike structure would be called the peduncle. (See Figures 2.1 and 2.2) A peduncle is the stem from which a phylum springs. Phyla grow and change over periods of time. After its initial emergence, the phylum goes through a period of rapid growth and change. Then it reaches a period of maturity where change slows down. Finally, through radial attraction there is a period of socialization and then a coming together into greater complexity. This is a critical period because at this point the phylum either closes over or a new peduncle emerges. If a new peduncle emerges, then evolution continues along this particular path of development. (See Figure 2.3) If the phylum closes over, then evolution has reached a dead end on this particular path of development. This same process repeats itself on every rung of the ladder of evolution all the way up to and including the human species.

The Tree of Life

Figure 2.1

An Individual Phylum

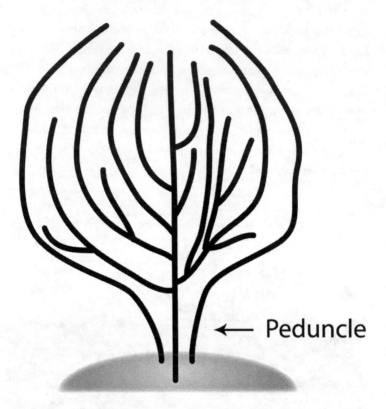

Figure 2.2

A New Peduncle Emerges

Figure 2.3

Teilhard believed that this pattern extends beyond biological evolution to include the evolution of consciousness. The network of living beings surrounding Earth is called the *biosphere*. It can be thought of as the layer of life surrounding Earth's surface. Teilhard hypothesized a similar sphere of *thought energy* surrounding Earth, which he termed the *noosphere*. This could be considered a living organism of collective human thought.

This noosphere is evolving. At the present time, the noosphere, the collective mind-stuff of the human race, has matured according to the pattern described for other phyla.

The noosphere is now at a stage of supersaturation. We are at a critical stage wherein this phylum will either close up into an evolutionary dead end or will produce a peduncle that takes us into the next phylum—beyond thought!

Teilhard emphasized that there is for us, in the future, under some form or another, not only the possibility of survival on Earth, but also *of a superior form of existence.* And he said that to imagine, discover and reach this superlife, we have only to *walk in the direction of the lines drawn by evolution.* We must understand these lines of evolution, how they operate, and then follow them to the next level.

Teilhard says that this will happen only if humankind becomes as a "collective human organism" drawn together by radial energy, that is, by love. "Man can hope for no evolutionary future except in association with all other men. Only by uniting can we progress. But this process must extend itself from simple reflective thought that is purely intellectual into a more complex form of thought ... sort of a hyperreflection."[13] As such, each person then becomes a supremely original center in which the universe uniquely reflects itself. These centers are our very selves. He referred to this state as the hyperpersonal.

Paradoxically, by uniting we achieve what Teilhard called a "supremely autonomous focus of union." We become individual grains of hyperconsciousness, in which union actually differentiates.[14] With every organized whole the parts perfect and fulfill themselves. As we move toward Omega in union with all others, we become more individuated, not less!

When viewed solely from the exterior, we see the universe moving toward a slow death through entropy. But when we view the interior world, we get a very different picture. We see the lines of evolution converging, somewhere ahead of us in time, into what Teilhard calls Omega: God, the One.

Structures of Consciousness

The leading edge of evolution is not in the biosphere, at the level of form, but in the noosphere, at the level of consciousness. For this reason, we are particularly interested in the structures of human consciousness within this noosphere.

We begin with the work of a little-known genius by the name of Jean Gebser. Gebser was born 1905 in Posen, Germany. He left Germany in 1929, lived in Italy, France and then Spain, where he participated in the Spanish Civil War. From there, he moved to Paris and then fled to Switzerland in 1939, barely escaping the Nazi invasion. The rest of his life was spent in Switzerland, where he did most of his writing. Jean Gebser was a philosopher, a scientist, a mystic and a published poet. His opus is titled *The Ever-Present Origin*, first published in 1949. He died in 1973.

Central to his work is the notion of the origin: the original impulse of life. He begins the preface to *The Ever-Present Origin* with these words: "Origin is ever-present. It is not a beginning, since all beginning is linked with time. And the present is not just the "now," today, the moment, or a unit of time. It is ever-originating, an achievement of full integration and continuous renewal."[15]

All structures of consciousness are animated by the origin itself. Gebser conceptualized these structures by how they lead us to experience the world itself. Each structure has its unique outlook, its unique way of interpreting reality; in particular, perceptions of space and time change from structure to structure.

Gebser described five major structures: *archaic, magic, mythical, mental* and *integral*. These structures are evolutionary; that is, they emerged over periods of time in hierarchic fashion. Each stage transcends but includes its previous stage; and there was often overlap between two of them in any given historic period.

The *archaic structure* is essentially prehuman, dating back about 5 million years to the first hominoids in Africa. This is at the dawn of self-awareness, but the light of awareness is still quite dim. This period could be likened to the metaphorical time of the Garden of Eden, before mankind's "fall" into ego-awareness.

The first fully human mode of consciousness is referred to as the *magical structure of consciousness*. It likely emerged with the first homo sapiens about 200,000 years ago and continued to be the primary structure of consciousness up until about 10,000 or so years ago.

This structure sees the world as alive and magical. Individual awareness is minimal; primary identity is with the tribe or the clan. Unlike his predecessor, the magical human is able to minimally distinguish himself from nature, yet he is still very much a part of nature. He interacts with nature through the medium of magic; this is the means of controlling his world.

Humans within this magical structure are unable to differentiate between subject and object. Anthropologist Sir James Frazer identified two fundamental principles of magical consciousness: 1. *The law of similarity:* that is, similarity is confused with identity. For example, every member of a particular clan is seen as the same individual; if one member commits a crime, then any other member of that clan can be punished as if they were the one that did it. 2. *The law of contagion:* proximity is confused with identity; any part can be confused with the whole.[16] For example, the bone of an animal could be seen to contain the full power of the animal; hence the use of amulets and talismans.

The next structure is known as the *mythical structure of consciousness*. Arising 10,000 to 15,000 years ago, this structure generally coincides with the beginning of recorded history; here is the advent of the agrarian culture, bringing with it commerce, metal-lurgy and art.[17]

The fertility goddesses were among the first of the mythic images. The later ascension of the male gods and the emergence of a supreme god created tension with the former goddess cults. Many stories in the Hebrew Bible focus on this tension. When Moses returned from the mountaintop after receiving instructions from Yahweh, the supreme god (who was male and lived in the sky), he found the people worshipping an icon of a golden calf, a common symbol in the fertility cults. Moses was not happy, nor was the Lord. Yahweh's very first commandment is "I am the Lord your God ... You shall have no other gods before me" (Ex. 20:2-3).

Human culture originated with this structure of conscious-ness. Culture is a shared story, a shared mythology. When we belong to a particular culture, we are members of that culture's mythology; we share in it and it makes us who we are. With this structure, economic power first emerged, and then political and military power. Kings and kingdoms emerged as part of the mythic structure, as did religions and priests. Priests and kings were earthly agents of a god who was now more abstract and dis-tant than ever before.

Around 500 BCE the *mental structure of consciousness* emerged in Greece and flourished in the Greek and Roman Civilization for many centuries. With the fall of Rome, it was largely lost in Europe for the next thousand years, replaced by the mythic con-sciousness during the so-called Dark Ages and the Middle Ages. The mental structure of consciousness resurfaced with the Renaissance in the 15th century, and it is the dominant mode of consciousness in the world today.

This consciousness structure is the modern self-reflective ego system. From it we have birthed science and created Western Civilization. Religion, art, literature, philosophy and politics all underwent great transformations when this structure was established as the dominant mode. Objectivity began to take on a new meaning as the ego identified its location as a point separated and distanced from the rest of the world.[18]

By separating our self from the world we were able to observe and analyze it and eventually to control it in ways undreamed of in prior eras. Our sense of self no longer resided in the body but in the head. As we gained the ability to control nature, we became more isolated from it.

In the prior chapter, I addressed some of the consequences of this worldview. With this mental structure, we have created the best and the worst of worlds. Gebser saw little hope for humankind's future if we remained here much longer. For him, the hope for the future lies in the emergence of the next structure.

The next structure, now in its incipiency, is the *integral, or aperspectival, structure of consciousness*. One of the characteristics of this structure is its perspective of time. In the mythic structure, there was a definite sense of past and future, but it was vague, imprecise, imbued with mythology. With the mental structure, time becomes an abstract linear quality. With the integral structure of consciousness, time is experienced as a holistic eternal presence, as exemplified by William Blake's familiar line "to see eternity in an hour."

A corresponding shift occurs in the view of the material world. In the mental structure, the world is distant and consists of inert matter. In the aperspectival structure, the material world becomes transparent, fluid and alive. The universe is seen as suffused with the light of the spirit, animated with the radiance of the ever present origin.

For Gebser, each structure sees the world through the phenomenon of projection, that is, the world that appears outside of us is actually a reflection of our own unseen self, which is projected, like a movie, onto our exterior world. With each progressive stage of evolution, there is a retraction of projected consciousness from the world. What seemed to be in the world is within ourselves. The world is evolving because we are evolving.[19]

The Gebserian term *aperspectival* is chosen to mean that this structure of consciousness, unlike the previous structures, is not limited to a singular perspective. From the mental structure, we see everything from our egoic perspective; we view it from our "point of view." Aperspectival consciousness is not limited to, or identified with, a particular point of view. Here we see things as they are rather than as we are. Some scholars believe that this should not be considered a perspective at all but rather "an open and fluid condition of being."[20]

Gebser strongly believed that the evolution to integral consciousness was absolutely necessary for humanity to survive. He also believed that it would not be easy. In 1949 he wrote: "If mankind can endure the new tensions that are becoming acute … then the impending collapse will only mean the end of the exclusive validity of the hitherto dominant mental structure. But if man and the earth are unable to endure these tensions, they will be torn apart by them."[21] According to Gebser, if we are willing to let go of the old worldview, then the evolutionary shift, though challenging, can be achieved. If we are not willing to let it go, then the results may be catastrophic.

Spiral Dynamics

Spiral Dynamics is a theory of human development introduced in the 1996 book *Spiral Dynamics* by Don Beck and Chris Cowan. This book is an extension and application of the work of Clare W. Graves. Graves, born in 1914, was professor of psychology at Union College in Schenectady, New York. He was deeply influenced by the work of the pioneer Humanistic psychologist Abraham Maslow.

Graves developed a model of human psychology, which he called "The Emergent Cyclical Levels of Existence Theory." Graves writes: "Briefly, what I am proposing is that the psychology of the mature human being is an unfolding, emergent, oscillating, spiraling process marked by progressive subordination of older, lower-behavior systems to newer higher order systems as man's existential problems change."[22]

Graves was a mentor for Don Beck, who has popularized and applied Graves work in the form of Spiral Dynamics. He has successfully applied this work in the areas of business, government, environment, international relations and a number of social and political arenas. He refers to Spiral Dynamics as a powerful tool for managing large-scale interventions, change and transformation.

To begin we must define the word *meme*. The word was first introduced by British scientist Richard Dawkins to discuss evolutionary principles in explaining the spread of ideas and cultural phenomena. A meme may be thought of as the cultural equivalent of a gene that can self-replicate and evolve through environmental pressure. Memes pattern the way we think, feel and act. Value memes are systems of core values that shape human choices and perspectives.

Graves has identified eight core value memes. The first six memes are referred to as the first tier memes, the second two as the second tier memes. These tiers roughly correspond with Maslow's distinction between deficiency needs and being needs. This idea will be developed as we explore the individual memes.

These memes developed in an evolutionary fashion, with each developing meme transcending and including its predecessor. Each of these memes has predominated during various periods of human history; and each developed to balance the missing elements in the prior meme. Although this system (as far as we know) developed independently of the previous evolutionary systems, we can readily see many parallels and commonalities.

The Memes

Each meme is identified by a color as well a name. We begin with the Beige Meme, which is referred to as the *Instinctive/Survivalistic Meme*. The name basically tells it all. This meme is about survival through the use of instinctual and habitual behaviors. "Do what you must do just to stay alive." The distinct self is barely awakened. This meme emerged about 100,000 years ago. This meme is essentially nonexistent today except for isolated instances.

The next meme is Purple, *the Magical/Animistic Meme*. Beginning about 50,000 years ago, this meme focuses on safety, which is largely accomplished by keeping the spirits appeased and happy. "Keep the spirits happy and the tribe safe." Individual identity is totally subsumed by tribal identification. The world is related to through magic and rituals. Great power is given to tribal leaders and to shamans. Ancestors are honored and often worshipped.

Today this meme is seen in the world's few remaining tribal cultures and in some developing nations in Africa, Asia and the Middle East. In the developed world this meme appears in isolated pockets. It appears primarily in the form of tribal loyalties, magic or superstition. We may see it operative within athletic teams, gangs or the mafia. It is estimated that 5 to 10 percent of the world's population functions in this meme.

The next meme is Red, *the Impulsive/Egocentric Meme*. This is the first emergence of the individual ego emerging from the collective tribal consciousness. And it erupts with vengeance: warlords, conquerors, feudal empires arise, and power gods dominate religious worship. "Be what you are and do what you want." Amoral behavior is common: instant gratification with no remorse is typical. Respect through domination is highly valued. This meme first emerged about 10,000 years ago. This meme exists today in parts of Africa, Asia and the Middle East. In the news media, it is often exemplified through warfare, terrorism and genocide. It exists in developed countries as the culture of urban gangs, neo-Nazi movements, motorcycle gangs and certain athletic contests. An estimated 15 to 20 percent of the world's population functions in this meme.

The next meme is Blue, *the Purposeful/Authoritarian Meme*. "Life has meaning, direction and purpose with predetermined outcomes." It emerged about 5,000 years ago in response to the anarchy and exploitive nature of the Red Meme. Sacrifice of self to a higher cause is highly valued. Absolute principles and rules must be followed. Impulsivity is controlled through guilt. Fundamentalism and patriotism abound. The hymn "Onward Christian Soldiers" exemplifies this meme, as does "The Battle Hymn of the Republic."

Blue is the most common meme in our world today. It exists in every developed nation and is the predominant meme in many of them. Emphasis is on stability and order; sacrifice brings future rewards. Reliance is upon authority and tradition as arbiters of truth and morality. Many military conflicts in the world today are between the Red and the Blue Memes vying for dominance. An estimated 35 to 40 percent of the world's population falls within this meme and about 25 percent of the U.S. population.

The next meme is Orange, *the Achiever/Strategic Meme*. First emerging about 400 years ago, this is the meme of science, capitalism and democracy. Individual achievement, objective inquiry and self-reliance are highly valued. Strategic risk-taking, creativity and prosperity are highly desirable. This is the dominant meme in most developed nations, including the United States. "Life, liberty and the pursuit of happiness" rules the day for Orange.

Conflicts between the Blue and Orange Memes abound in the United States. The creationism versus evolution debate is a classic Blue-Orange battle, wherein Blue invokes Divine Authority as the source of truth and Orange uses scientific inquiry and reason as its criterion of what is true. Likewise with abortion and euthanasia issues: Blue sees these as serious moral infractions, but Orange sees the issue to be the right of every individual to have a choice.

Orange constitutes about 30 percent of the world's population and about 50 percent of the United States. Though it is not the most common meme in the world today, it is by far the most powerful. It impacts virtually all people on planet Earth today—for better or worse.

The next meme is Green, *the Communitarian/Egalitarian Meme.* "Seek peace with the inner self and explore, with others, the caring dimensions of community." Although it's very first emergence was in the mid-19th century, the Green Meme really "made the scene" in the 1960s. The cold rationality of Orange was challenged with Green's emphasis on warmth, sensitivity and caring. A new form of spirituality emerged in response to the dogmatism that often developed in Blue. The excesses of capitalism were met with a desire to share Earth's resources with all and to ensure that everyone has equal opportunity to meet basic material needs. The emphasis is on inclusiveness; decision-making is done through consensus. Authenticity, openness, harmony, equality and sensitivity are highly valued.

Orange and Green have clashed on issues such as environmental concerns versus economic concerns (logging, for example) and issues of equal opportunity employment versus the economic needs of the business community. Blue-Green clashes may focus around issues such as gay rights or anti-war demonstrations. The highest concentration of the Green Meme in the world is in Western Europe, particularly Scandinavia. Only 10 percent of Earth's population is at Green; but about 25 percent of the United States is Green. In recent years, we have seen trends toward Orange—and even Blue—becoming "tinged" with Green, particularly in the environmental and human rights arenas.

Second Tier

As mentioned previously, the memes are divided into two tiers. Green is the highest level in the first tier. But, before we go any further, let's get clear on what we mean by "higher and lower." These words are often considered to be "downright sinful" in our postmodern egalitarian culture, so let's look carefully.

Most school systems categorize students by higher and lower grades, such as first grade, second grade and so on. In this context, a "higher" grade simply means that the students have passed through all of the preceding grades. Higher does not mean superior in any absolute sense. Higher education does not necessarily mean superior education; it simply means education aimed at a different level of development. "Higher" simply means having developmentally progressed through the previous stages.

Now everyone at Green has progressed through all the prior first tier stages, and to progress beyond Green is to move into "second tier." A primary difference between first and second tier is that each first tier meme sees itself as right, and the others as wrong, or at least misguided. With each progression up the ladder there is increasing recognition and tolerance for other perspectives, but even Green sees itself as essentially right and the other memes as "less enlightened." Even the view that "there is no one right answer" believes itself to be "the right answer."

Second tier might be termed "metaperspectives." That is, we see every perspective as simply a perspective; we are not identified with any one of them. Second tier is readily able to see through the eyes of another.

To illustrate, we use an adapted version of the oft-told Hindu story of the elephant and the three blind men. As the story goes, one blind man grabs the tail of the elephant and he imagines the elephant as a very long rope. A second touches the side of the elephant and he imagines the elephant to be a big wall. A third grabs a leg of the elephant, and he imagines the elephant to be a big tree. The three later convene to discuss what an elephant is, but they quickly get into a big argument because each one was locked into his own image of an elephant and refused to give validity to the viewpoint of the others.

Now a second tier blind man would listen to the accounts of his friends, but rather than argue with them he would be able to construct a composite picture of the elephant in his own mind, because he knows that each person, including himself, has but a partial view, and that each view is as valid or invalid as the others. By being able to go beyond his personal perspective, he can acquire knowledge that is impossible to achieve through any singular perspective by itself.

As mentioned previously, Clare Graves was strongly influenced by Abraham Maslow, who identified tiers of human needs. He named the first type *deficiency needs* and the second type *being needs*. A deficiency need arises because of a perceived emptiness or deficiency within oneself. For example, the need for love arises when we feel a deficiency of love within us, so we seek it from another. Conversely, a being need arises simply because one's fullness of being requires expression. For example, the creative urge arises to express oneself through art, poetry and so on.

In the second tier memes, there is an openness of being, a quality of being able to flow with life and adapt to changing circumstances, yet still be able to function optimally. Many believe that development to this level by a sufficient number of people is essential for the next step in our evolution. At present, Beck estimates that less than 2 percent of the world's population is at second tier.

In reviewing the memes, we see that every other meme is either a *Self* Meme or an *Us* Meme. The Self Memes are Beige, Red, Orange and (second tier) Yellow. The Us Memes are Purple, Blue, Green and (second tier) Turquoise. Each meme emerges to balance the bias of the prior meme. When a Self Meme becomes overdeveloped or out of balance, then the next meme that emerges to restore balance is an Us Meme and vice versa. Each Self Meme that emerges is more mature than the prior Self Meme because it has passed through the intervening Us Meme. For example, the ego energy of Red is used in Orange, but it is more mature and focused on more productive and beneficial outcomes than is Red. This continues to an even greater degree with Yellow. Likewise with the Us Memes. And so goes our evolution.

As with all evolutionary patterns, each stage will transcend but include each of the previous memes. We carry all of the memes within us. When we are stressed, there is a tendency to revert to a prior mode of functioning. For example, someone at Green may revert to Blue or Red behavior under crisis conditions.

Each meme has its healthy and unhealthy (shadow) expression. The best way for us to facilitate growth into the next higher meme is to become healthy within the existing meme. For example, the best way to progress from Green to Yellow is to become a healthy Green, but to not be overly identified with this value system. We will explore this idea in greater detail in a later chapter.

The Bible as a Story of Evolution

The place we go for our last evolutionary map is the last place most people would go to study evolution: the Bible. Charles and Myrtle Fillmore, founders of the Unity movement, used the Bible as a metaphorical framework for studying the growth and development of consciousness. They studied the Bible as history and allegory and interpreted it as a metaphysical representation of humankind's evolutionary journey toward spiritual awakening.[23] The Fillmores began their work in 1889, in Kansas City, Missouri. They were widely read in many traditions, including Eastern philosophy and many esoteric teachings, but they used Christianity as the foundation for their work of spiritual education. The teachings of Jesus formed the core of their New Thought Christianity. The Bible, interpreted metaphysically, was seen as a foundational framework for their teachings.

Metaphysical interpretation is a perspective wherein every character, place and object in a Bible story is seen as the representation of some aspect of our personal or collective consciousness at some stage of development. The relationship of these characters and the drama that unfolds within a Bible story is the metaphorical representation of developmental processes unfolding within consciousness. By interpreting these stories metaphysically and meditating upon them, one can learn much about the evolution of human consciousness.

Viewing the Bible as a whole, we see two basic sets of writings, each of which write about, and were written in, different historical periods. Formerly called the Old and the New Testaments, they are now commonly referenced in scholarly circles as the Hebrew Bible and the Christian Bible. However, we will use the terms Old Testament and New Testament simply because that terminology more accurately reflects our evolutionary focus on the Bible.

Reviewing some of the maps we have considered thus far, we see a progression of evolutionary development of consciousness stretching into the distant past and bringing us to the present and into the future. We can see the Bible as such a map. We see the Bible as symbolically representing humankind's journey from subconsciousness to consciousness to superconsciousness. The subconscious contains memories and patterns laid down in our past—both our personal past and our collective past. The super-conscious is that aspect of mind that contains potential that may unfold in the future, and perhaps *must* unfold.[24]

Generally speaking, the Old Testament symbolizes the progression from the subconscious to consciousness, that is, the past to the present. The New Testament symbolizes the progression from consciousness to superconsciousness. Metaphysically interpreted, the Bible contains both a map of our past and a blueprint for our future.

Historically, the Old Testament covers a period from about 1900 BCE, with the call of Abraham, to about 1250 BCE with the death of Moses. The Old Testament narrative begins with the creation story, which includes our friend Adam—whose name in Hebrew means "human." We see Adam as symbolic of the primal human living unconsciously in the garden of nature. I don't believe that early humans lived in paradise because archeological evidence suggests that they lived very short lives and were often ridden with disease—not to mention the hardship of living at the mercy of nature. However, they did deeply identify with nature, especially in religious worship and ritual, because they were dependent upon nature for their survival. The "garden" is symbolic of the primal innocence of the pre-egoic consciousness. In this garden there is no knowledge of good and evil, right and wrong. Life was far from easy, but early humans probably did not suffer from the existential angst that plagues most moderns.

Adam's expulsion from the garden is symbolic of this "fall" from innocence. Historically, it could represent the period beginning with the use of agriculture—which generally coincides with the commencement of written history. This is what Gebser called the *mythic structure of consciousness*, wherein we see the beginning of commerce and the trappings of civilization.

The Old Testament character Abraham symbolizes the initial stirrings of spiritual consciousness. He was called by the Lord to fulfill his destiny as the Patriarch, the Father of the Hebrew people. Abraham lived in the period when the Blue Meme of Spiral Dynamics had just begun to emerge. "Life has meaning, direction and purpose with predetermined outcomes" is a major premise of the Blue Meme.

The historic period of the Old Testament concludes with the story of Moses. Moses was a primal Christ figure. The story of his birth in Egypt, wherein he had to be hidden from Pharaoh (symbolic of the ruling ego), parallels the story of Jesus' birth. Jesus had to be hidden, taken to Egypt, to avoid being killed by King Herod, who also represents the egoic consciousness. Both stories portray the archetype of the divine child, whose appearance portends a transformation of consciousness that will subsume the former ego-based awareness. The ego seeks to destroy this divine child at every opportunity.

Moses communed with the Lord and received the Law that was part of the covenant the Lord created with His people. Moses symbolizes the level of consciousness that is clearly spiritually based, but functions primarily through the law of cause and effect. Once again, this is classic Blue Meme functioning: Reliance is upon authority and tradition as arbiters of truth and morality; emphasis is on stability and order, sacrifice brings future rewards.

In the Old Testament the relationship between God and man is that of creator to creature. The primary work of humanity in this period was to know and obey God's laws. This paradigm not only represents a level of consciousness that predominated in the past, but one that still predominates in much of the world today; it exists in all of us to some degree.

The New Testament begins with John the Baptist "crying in the wilderness," warning people to repent and prepare for the kingdom of heaven. John wore rough clothing, ate raw food, and spoke the plain truth. Sometimes he spoke in a very critical and reactive manner. He could readily see the shortcomings of the Jewish religious establishment, but he never quite saw the kingdom of heaven itself.

John is symbolic of the illumined intellect, which can sense the onset of spiritual awakening and can see the error of our present ways but cannot fully comprehend the truth that it is promoting. John is the spiritual intellect at its best; this can be exemplified by many scholars and preachers who do a wonderful job of speaking *about the truth* but are be unable to personally experience it.

Jesus said, "You shall know the truth and the truth shall set you free" (Jn. 8:32). The "knowing" to which he was referring was not an intellectual knowing, but a *gnosis*; a knowing that penetrates into the depths of one's soul; a knowing that does not inform, but transforms. John, the intellect, is not capable of this level of knowing.

The early New Testament represents the conscious mind that is capable of anticipating and preparing for the superconscious but cannot go there. Jesus, the central character of the New Testament, symbolizes the superconscious, the vehicle for our experience of truth: "I am the way, the truth and the life" (Jn. 14:6).

Moses symbolizes the letter of the law; Jesus symbolizes the spirit of the law. With Jesus, humankind was elevated from being simply a creature to becoming a co-creator. Moses tells us that our work is to understand the law and to obey God; Jesus tells us that our work is to know God, to serve God, and ultimately, to become one with God. "The Father and I are one" (Jn. 10:30).

In the Old Testament, the city of Jerusalem is established as the capital of Israel when King David brought the Ark of the Covenant into the city. Jerusalem, which means "city of peace," has since been the holy city of Judaism. Today it is the holy city for three religions: Judaism, Christianity and Islam. At the close of the New Testament, in the book of Revelation, reference is made to the New Jerusalem:

> Then I saw a new heaven and a new earth: for the first heaven and the first earth had passed away .... And I saw the holy city, the new Jerusalem, coming down out of heaven.... And I heard a loud voice from the throne saying, "See, the home of God is among mortals. He will dwell with them as their God; they will be his peoples, and God himself shall be with them (Rev. 21:1-3).

Here we have a biblical description of what Teilhard might call the Omega Point, the time and place when all sense of separation between God and man has ceased. Thus the Bible can be seen as pointing our evolution in the same direction as that of the many scientists, philosophers and visionaries that we have studied here.

In Summary

1. For humans, biological evolution is essentially over. There will be no further evolution without conscious evolution.

2. We consider evolution as having purpose, and that all of life is being drawn toward that purpose. Evolution is not just about the past but also the future.

3. The purpose of evolution is for the Absolute to unfold itself within the relative universe. Human history is the Absolute unfolding through the consciousness of humanity.

4. To understand evolution, we must understand involution. With involution, Spirit involves itself in its creation: Spirit loses itself in its creation so it can find itself through evolution. That loss is entirely in appearance, not in reality. With each descent down the Great Chain, Spirit becomes identified with that level.

5. In evolution, Spirit unfolds that which it enfolded in involution. It "ascends" by transforming into the next level of the Great Chain. Through evolution, Spirit "remembers" what was "lost" in involution.

6. Henri Bergson argued that evolution is propelled by a force—the *élan vital*—which is consciousness itself. The élan vital operates through evolution into ever higher levels of expression thereby freeing consciousness from the constriction of matter.

7. Teilhard de Chardin believed that nature has two faces: the exterior face of matter, and the interior reality, or consciousness. The evolution of complexity in the physical world is accompanied by evolution in the quality and the degree of consciousness in the interior world. He called this the Law of Complexity-Consciousness.

8. Teilhard recognized two forms of energy: tangential energy, the external component; and radial energy, the internal

component that moves all things toward greater complexity-consciousness. He equated radial energy with love.

9. Teilhard emphasized that we will not only survive but will evolve into a superior form of existence. He said to reach this superlife we have to walk in the direction of the lines drawn by evolution. He saw the lines of evolution converging, somewhere ahead of us in time, into what he calls Omega.

10. He said this would happen only if humankind became a "collective human organism" drawn together by radial energy, that is, by love. Only by uniting can we progress. As we move toward Omega in union with all others, we become *more* individuated, not less: each person becomes a center in which the universe uniquely reflects itself.

11. Jean Gebser sees structures of consciousness animated by the origin itself. These structures shape our experience of the world; each has its unique way of interpreting reality. He described five major structures: *archaic, magic, mythical, mental* and *integral*. These structures emerged over periods of time in hierarchic fashion; each stage transcends but includes its previous stage.

12. The mental structure is the self-reflective ego system. Through it we have created the best and the worst of worlds. Gebser saw little hope for humankind's future if we remain here. The hope for the future lies in emergence of the next structure.

13. This next structure is the *integral,* or *aperspectival,* structure of consciousness. Here the material world becomes transparent, fluid and alive; the universe is seen as suffused with the light of the spirit. Gebser believed that the evolution to *integral* is necessary for humanity to survive.

14. According to Gebser, each structure sees through projection; the world that appears outside of us is a reflection of our own unseen self. With each progressive stage there is a retraction of

projected consciousness from the world. What seemed to be in the world is within us.

15. A meme is the cultural equivalent of a gene. Value memes are core values that shape human choices and perspectives. They pattern the way we think, feel and act. Clare Graves identified eight core value memes. The first six memes are first tier memes, the second two are second tier memes. These memes developed in an evolutionary fashion. Each meme emerges to balance the bias of the prior meme.

16. A primary difference between first and second tier is that each first tier meme sees itself as "right" and others as "wrong." At second tier we see every perspective as simply a perspective; we are not identified with any one of them. Many believe that development to this level is the next step in our evolution.

17. The Bible may be seen as symbolically representing humankind's journey from subconsciousness to consciousness to superconsciousness. The superconscious is that aspect of mind that contains unrealized potential that can unfold in the future.

18. The Old Testament symbolizes the progression from the subconscious to consciousness, that is, the past to the present. The New Testament symbolizes the progression from consciousness to superconsciousness, present to future. Metaphysically interpreted, the Bible contains a map of our past and a potential blueprint for our future.

Segue

We have gleaned many useful insights from some of the most brilliant minds to have considered the topic of the evolution of consciousness. So far we have focused on phylogenic evolution, which is the evolution of a particular species: Homo sapiens sapiens. To progress further in our exploration, we will focus upon *ontogenic evolution,* that is, the development of the individual. Our exploration of the evolution of consciousness continues.

3

A Case of Mistaken Identity

A s we explore the evolution of consciousness, we must consider the development of each individual as a center of consciousness. Evolution occurs one person at a time. The structures of consciousness that we discussed in the last chapter exist only because individual human beings embody these structures. Even Teilhard's *noosphere*, which may metaphorically be considered a sphere of thought surrounding the earth, does not exist within space, but only within consciousness.

The future of the human race is influenced by each of us in every moment. It is time for evolution to become conscious; our survival depends upon this. We can no longer look to some power outside of ourselves to save us from our own ignorance. Conscious evolution means that we grow up; we are no longer merely children of God: We are now partners and co-creators with the divine.

Conscious evolution now requires us to evolve beyond the present level of ego identification. To evolve beyond this level, we must see how we became *involved* within it. Involution is not just an event that occurred long ago; it recurs with the birth of every living being. You are Spirit that has involved itself into matter and evolved itself into human form. You are Spirit calling itself *me*.

Who Am I?

So then, who, or what, is this being called *me*? Who am I? Well, I might begin by saying that "I am this body." I certainly identify with a particular physical form. I look in the mirror and I say, "That one's me!"

But is this physical form my deepest identification? Do I, like most animals, spend most of my time feeding, defending and protecting my physical body? Probably not; I, like most people, spend much more time feeding, defending and protecting some invisible entity that lives somewhere within this body—namely, in the head. Fortunately, it is fairly rare that my body feels threatened, but this entity inside of my head feels threatened much of the time! I put a lot of energy into its care and feeding, and its safety and security.

I am referring to what many would call the *ego*. It is the ego, not the body that gets most of our attention. In fact, many of us will neglect or mistreat the body in order to satisfy the ego.

The word *ego* is Latin for "I." So let's explore this "I." If someone asks, "Who are you?" we typically respond by sharing factual data such as name, gender, nationality and so on. "I am Robert, a male, an American." This is fine for social conversation, but in truth there could be several people who fit the description I just provided, but they are not me. So what is it that makes me, *me*?

I could describe psychological characteristics: introvert, intuitive, intelligent and so forth. But once again, these are simply descriptive categories not unique to me. They may be helpful at times, but they don't answer the question "Who am I?"

I can speak theologically and say "I am a soul" or "I am a spirit," but these are terms which identify categories of being.

They may be helpful in describing *what* I am, but they do not define *who* I am.

If I say, "I am an expression of God," then I must give you a definition of God, and I must tell you who or what exists that is *not* an expression of God—otherwise my response has no meaning. If *everyone* is an expression of God, then I haven't told you anything about who *I* am.

I can say, "Let me tell you more about myself," and then add, "I like pizza, baseball and jazz. My best friends are Tom, Jerry and Suzy. I am committed to improving the world." Now we are getting a bit more personal because we are going beyond categories describing *me* to identifying my values and my desires. This may give you a more personal sense of me, but who is the *me* that has these desires and values?

I can speak existentially and state, "Who I am is my experience in this moment." I can then define my present moment experience: "I am seeing this and I am feeling that and I am thinking this." But you could then ask me, "*Who* is it that is seeing, feeling, thinking? Who is it that is having these experiences that you are describing?"

This exploration is analogous to you entering a very dark room with a flashlight in hand and slowly searching every square inch of the room with the flashlight beam. Eventually you will see everything in that room ... except for one thing. You will never see the *source of the light*—the flashlight.

> Once upon a time there lived a king who possessed a sword that was said to be so sharp that it could cut anything on earth. The king challenged anyone in his kingdom to bring him something which the sword could not cut. Many persons brought objects of every variety: iron, stones and even diamonds, but the sword easily cut through each of them.

> Finally, a young lad stood before the king and said, "Your Excellency, I can name the one thing which your sword can never cut." The king replied: "Impossible! Show me." The boy simply pointed to the sword in the king's own hand: the sword cannot cut itself.

The self is forever the subject. When we try to see the self as an object it disappears. It's like trying to see the back of your head; it forever eludes you.

When I ask, "Who am I?" I could follow with the question "*Who* is it that is asking 'Who am I?'" Which in turn could be followed by the question "*Who* is it that is asking 'Who is it that is asking who am I?'" This process could go on forever—it is an infinite regress. It is like holding two mirrors in front of each other: We see an infinite series of images of me looking at me looking at me ...

"I" disappears in the very searching for it. We can never find this "I" because it is the subject that is looking for itself as an object. And the subject is forever the subject; it can never be the object. The philosopher Alan Watts would often say that trying to locate this "I" is like "trying to bite your own teeth!"

> And then the young man said, "So,
> It would seem that I know that I know;
> But what I would like to see
> Is the me that sees me
> When I *know* that I know that I know."
>
> —Anonymous

Who I really am, who you really are, is forever a mystery to the mind. But the mind does not like mysteries; it wants answers. The mind wants certainty. To face the unknown is virtually intolerable for the mind. So the mind proceeds to identify the self in the only way that it knows how. And that way is given by the following illustration.

Imagine that you were given the task of describing a hole in a wall. You would likely begin by describing the location, size and shape of the hole. But someone could say, "Wait a minute, you aren't describing the hole; you are describing the wall that surrounds the hole. You are saying nothing about the hole itself." You might then look at the hole and describe what you see beyond the hole. But they could then respond, "You are not describing the hole itself, you are describing what is behind the hole." Eventually you might come to say, "I am describing this hole in the only way possible, by describing that which surrounds it."

This is the way the human mind answers the question, "Who am I?" It answers in the only way that it can. It cannot describe the hole itself so it describes that which surrounds the hole. This is the mind's way of identifying itself. We identify self by all that surrounds it, but we can never directly identify the self. Like the hole, it is indescribable in and of itself.

Knowing this limitation, we can still use the mind and its concepts and its words, but in a different way. Rather than using the mind to define the self, let's use the mind, and its tools, to *point to* the self. Words and concepts can be used as signposts that point to the destination but are not intended to be the destination itself. A sign pointing to New York City is not New York City, but it can help you to get there, so that you can experience the Big Apple directly for yourself.

More Trail Markers

We find accounts of individuals throughout history who seem to have experienced this true self beyond the mind. Some of the words left by these folks can be useful signposts. Going further, we can look at teachings given by those who have not only experienced the true self, but seem to have lived from it most of the time. These teachings are like trail markers from those who have traveled the path before us.

Throughout the world we find teachings of wisdom that seem remarkably similar, even though they originated in different places and at different periods of human history. We can readily find these teachings embedded within many Eastern religious scriptures and texts. In the West, this ancient wisdom has, until recently, been largely hidden from the average person's view.[25] Fortunately for us living today, the teachings from virtually every wisdom tradition throughout human history are readily available to us.

This ancient wisdom tells us that who we really are, our true nature, exists in a realm beyond time and space; that awareness becomes lost after Spirit incarnates in human form. Involution repeats itself with the birth of every human being. Wordsworth implies this in his poetry:

> Our birth is but a sleep and a forgetting:
> The Soul that rises with us, our life's Star,
> Hath elsewhere its setting,
> And cometh from afar.
> Not in entire forgetfulness,
> And not in utter nakedness,
> But trailing clouds of glory do we come
> From God, who is our home:
> Heaven lies about us in our infancy!
> Shades of the prison-house begin to close
> Upon the growing boy.
> But he beholds the light, and whence it flows,
> He sees it in his joy;
> The youth, who daily farther from the east
> Must travel, still is Nature's Priest,
> And by the vision splendid

Is on his way attended;
At length the man perceives it die away,
And fade into the light of common day.[26]

Identification becomes embedded first in the body, and then in the mind, so we gradually lose awareness of our identity as spirit and soul. The human mind can function only within the domain of time—it cannot go beyond this. It cannot grasp the source of itself beyond time anymore than the flashlight can see itself; thus there is a "black hole" in the mind's ability to know its origin.

Our personal identity—the ego—is a product of the mind, and the ego perceives this black hole as death itself. It perceives this hole as a huge void that will annihilate its identity. Therefore the ego will resist any attempt to enter this hole; in fact, it doesn't even want to admit that it exists.

The True Self

To discover what is within and beyond this hole we must venture beyond the realm of ordinary mind. We can do this by looking at reports of those who seem to have experienced the self that lies beyond the mind—beyond time and space. Those persons who have experienced this transcendent self (and there are very many) report that this self is *infinitely more real* that their personal identity.

Author Jean Houston writes of such an experience when she was a child: "I was no longer just ... Jean Houston, age 6 ... I had awakened to a consciousness that spanned centuries and was on intimate terms with the universe. Everything mattered. Nothing was alien or irrelevant or distant. The farthest star was right next door, and the deepest mystery was mystically seen. It seemed as if I knew everything, as if I was everything ...."[27]

We see parallels in this account by Alfred Lord Tennyson, the 19th-century English poet, who had many such experiences: "A kind of waking trance ... I have frequently had, quite up from boyhood, when I had been all alone ... All at once ... individuality itself seemed to dissolve and fade away into boundless being, and this ... the clearest, the surest of the surest, utterly beyond words .... The loss of personality (if it were so) seeming no extinction, but the only true life."[28]

This "only true life" to which Tennyson refers is the life that expresses itself in every human being, and indeed, in every life form on this planet. When we experience the reality of our true self, we know that there is no essential difference between this self and all that exists. The true self is Spirit itself. This is the central message of all ancient wisdom traditions. These teachings tell us that our true nature is Spirit—infinite and eternal—and that our sense of a separate self is actually an illusion created by the human mind. The subject-object duality created by the mind is a fiction.

In the ancient teaching of Vedanta, a philosophical school within Hinduism, there is a familiar aphorism—*Tat Tvam Asi*: Thou art That. All that I see—and much more—is in reality, my Self. Swami Vivekananda, a leading proponent of Vedanta, writes: "To every man this is taught: Thou art one with this universal being, and, as such, every soul that exists is your soul, and every body that exists is your body .... For I am the universe. This universe is my body."[29]

We are one with all that exists. A corollary to this principle can be expressed as follows: The cause of all of human suffering lies in the mistaken belief that our separated personal self is our true self and that it is real. This is humanity's case of mistaken identity. The only permanent end to human suffering lies in awakening to the truth of who we really are. This is the direction of conscious evolution.

Being in the World

A skeptic might protest: "Wait a minute! All this is wonderful indeed, but how can I possibly function in this world if I am always walking around being 'one with everything'? Wouldn't this lead to chaos and confusion?"

Ancient Wisdom might respond: "Perhaps, at first; but this awakening is a birth into a greater reality, and like our human birth, we need time to develop the skills required to function in this new dimension." Those who have had such an experience often report a brief period of disorientation, but eventually they learn to integrate this new awareness into their everyday life. Conscious evolution is not just transcending our existing level but also integrating all of our prior knowledge and understanding into this new reality.

Awakening to our true nature does not deny the fact that we must still function in the world as an individual. The difference is that, when awakened, we are no longer identified with being *only* an individual. This radically changes the way we live.

For illustration, let's use an analogy. Consider the human personality as being a block of ice. If identified exclusively with this block of ice, then we will live in constant fear that we may melt and cease to exist, or fear that we will be crushed into pieces and die. In addition, as a block of ice, we cannot easily merge with other pieces of ice; our edges are jagged and brittle. Intimacy is difficult because it touches our fear of melting or being crushed.

But let's say that this block of ice has a spiritual experience and discovers its true nature as H_2O. This block of ice will still exist as a separate entity, but because it knows that its true nature is H_2O, it no longer fears melting or being broken. Even if it were to melt or be crushed it still knows that its true nature—H_2O—remains unchanged. In the form of ice, water or vapor it still is its essential self. If it wishes to merge with other blocks of ice, it can melt into water and merge with delight. If it wishes to be invisible and unlimited, it can vanish into water vapor. If it wishes to be hard and solid, it can freeze back into a piece of ice. None of these changes affect its true nature, so it is free from its former fear. It is free to be whatever it needs to be at any given time.

So it is with the individual self that knows its essential nature as Spirit. This person can be as hard as ice, as fluid as water, or as spacious as vapor. She can function effectively as an individual in her day-to-day world and still know the truth of her unlimited nature. She can actually function with greater ease in her life because she is not using her energy to maintain and protect a false identity—as most of us do. She no longer fears intimacy. She does not even fear death because she knows that changes in form do not affect her true identity. Such a person is free to express her heart's deepest desire without fear of harm or destruction.

The Trailhead

But the vast majority of humanity is identified with the personal self and *do* experience themselves as separate and vulnerable. Some of these individuals are aware of this identification and desire to become free to experience their true nature. These persons are aware of that identification and are no longer seeking refuge in it. They have tasted the fruits of the ego and found it wanting. It is to these individuals that our words are primarily addressed.

The path to freedom begins with the realization that we are *not free* as we are living right now. To become conscious of one's separateness is to become conscious of one's suffering. This can give us a great incentive to engage the journey of awakening. In Ken Wilber's words, "As each level emerges, consciousness exclusively identifies with the substitute gratification until it has been tasted and found wanting."[30]

To become free of ego identification and to awaken to one's true nature, it is very helpful (and perhaps essential) to see how we have become ensnared in false self-identification and how we unconsciously *continue to ensnare ourselves*. The false self is not an object; it is not a thing. It is a process; it is something that we are *creating* virtually every moment. This false self is a pattern of repetitive thoughts, feelings and behaviors. It can exist only as this pattern is consistently reinforced; *it has no independent existence*. To become free, we need to recognize this pattern and see when and how we continue to reinforce it, and then stop reinforcing it.

Terminology

I want to be clear regarding terms that I use, because these terms are used in different ways by different authors. I use the term *personality* to denote the psychological structure of the individual. I use the term *essence*, or *essential nature*, to refer to Spirit operative as the core of each individual. This essence may also be referred to as *true nature* or *true self*. When we are spiritually awake, the personality serves as an instrument of essential nature, which is Spirit. The personality and the body are vehicles for essential nature as it functions in time and space.

The ego is that which we call "I" or "me." The ego is our conscious identity. With most of us, this "I" is exclusively identified with the personality; we believe ourselves *to be* the personality, and we believe that it is *real*. The ego then becomes a *false self*— because it is identified completely with the personality and is ignorant of essence.[31] With this false identification, essential nature is unable to fully express itself.

Rather than being a vehicle for essence, the personality then becomes an *obscuration* of essence. Because of ego's ignorance of essence, it feels vulnerable and fearful; the personality then becomes like a medieval suit of armor; it may appear to protect us, but it severely limits the expression of our true self.

As we evolve in the conscious awareness of our essential nature, the personality becomes more transparent and flexible; it gradually becomes a vehicle for essence rather than an obscuration. Ego identification eventually shifts toward the essence animating the personality, rather than the personality alone. We then function more effectively in the world because we no longer need to fearfully defend the personality-identified ego; as essence we are invulnerable and are able to function freely in our world. We are *in* the world but not *of* the world. We do not lose the ego—it is the sense of "I"—but the ego is surrendered to essence; it functions more like the butterfly than the caterpillar.

Why We Develop a False Self

The development of the false self, or ego's identification with personality, is virtually inevitable given that we were raised by human parents and a human family. The overwhelming majority of us were parented and nurtured by individuals who were identified with their personality—their false self. Our culture is characterized by this identification; it is considered normal at this stage in our evolution.

We are born originally identified with essence. As we grow from infancy to childhood, three primary factors influence the shift of identity from essence to personality. These factors shape the development of the false self. First is our identification with a physical body. This identification is normal and is largely in place by the end of our first year. A second factor, at work throughout childhood, is the experience of not having our needs adequately met. This may include traumas that intensify the identity shift from essence to personality. As a consequence, we develop a mental strategy for protecting ourselves from further trauma and from feeling the pain of primary needs going unmet. These strategies become habitual and eventually become part of our identity as a personality.

A third factor at work in developing the false self is the lack of essential mirroring. Essential mirroring is needed for essence to develop and integrate with the personality. This mirroring must occur in two directions. The parents must perceive the child's essence—which they can do only if they can perceive their own; the child must perceive it in the parents. For essence to develop within the child, she must first perceive it in her primary caregivers; this perception will stimulate development of her own essential nature. For her own essential nature to be recognized by the child, she must see it reflected in the significant people in her life.

Most likely our parents were unaware of their own essential nature and were unable to model it for us or to see it within us. Most likely, our essential nature was not reflected back to us; therefore it could not fully develop. To compensate for our undeveloped essence, we developed a mental strategy for getting what we needed from the world around us. This survival strategy became a substitute for awareness of our essential nature; thus we identified with personality.

For example, my father never learned to trust his own heart; he relied almost completely upon an external authority for his deepest sense of truth. By contrast, as a young boy, I often felt guided by an "inner knowing" that led me in positive directions. As I grew older, I would sometimes verbally share this internal process with my parents. I often felt them respond with a subtle, yet strong sense of disapproval. I was often asked how I thought I knew certain things or why I acted in ways that seemed counter to what they called "common sense." Out of my need for their approval, I unconsciously distanced myself from this inner knowing and learned to rely exclusively upon "rational" or "objective" measures for choices that I made. Many years later I would feel the pain of this disowned part of myself.

How We Develop a False Self

We are born, as Wordsworth says, "trailing clouds of glory." These clouds of glory may well be the radiance of our essential nature. Since the personality has not yet formed there is little to obscure this essence. This may be why we are attracted to infants and young children; they exude a certain radiance and purity that remind us of that lost part of ourselves.

Yet this little bundle of essence does not have the ability to survive in the physical world in its present form. As humans, we have relatively few innate survival instincts; instead we survive by internalizing that which we learn from our early life experiences. This training is provided by our parents, caregivers and role models, whether they realize it or not. The human mind is a product of our evolution; it was designed for our survival, just as every other animal has evolved its tools for survival. But with humans our primary survival tools are passed on via family and culture rather than DNA.

We begin this life physically and psychically embedded within our mother. After about nine months in utero we separate physically from her, but we remain psychically embedded with her for several more months. Then we begin a process of differentiation. This process is gradual and complex, but sometime during our third year of life most of us develop a sense of self. We do this largely by "internalizing" our mother. Eventually this internal mother will become more influential than the external one.

In the meantime, this separate self continues to develop, gradually finding ways to get her needs met apart from external mom. Her survival becomes less and less dependent upon Mom. It is via this process of separation and internalization that the child gradually develops an independent self, a personality.

Personality Development

The human personality develops so that we can survive and function in the world. Earlier we addressed our human dilemma of living with two conflicting drives: the drive to survive as a separate entity and the drive to experience our true self, to be all that we are capable of becoming. Our deepest need is to experience our essential nature, but this need is usually trumped by our survival needs.

Implicit in the development of a healthy personality is the fulfillment of our basic human needs. Needs are universal human desires; they exist in virtually every human being and within every culture. A certain degree of fulfillment of these needs is necessary for a child to develop a healthy personality. As children we need food, water and sleep. We require clothing, shelter and a sense of safety. We need to feel loved and to bond with others. We need to have a certain sense of autonomy and self-esteem. If these needs are not adequately met, the personality will not develop optimally.

Ideally, children would have no conflict between expressing their essential nature and having their human needs met. They could be who we truly are and have all of their human needs fulfilled. In this perfect world, personality is integrated with essential nature and is an expression of it.

If all of our needs are recognized and met by parents who are consciously attuned to their essential nature, then this may be possible.[32] When parents are consciously attuned to their own essence, they are able to perceive their child's essential nature. This recognition and mirroring supports the development of essence within the child. As the child's needs are met with her essential nature recognized and supported, the personality will develop as a natural expression of the essential nature. The child develops an inherent faith in life and in herself; she learns to rely upon her own essential nature to function in this world.

But this is very rare. Most often our needs were not met in this way. Most likely, our parents were imperfect human beings who lived ignorant of their own essential nature; they were probably identified with their personality. As such, they were most likely wounded by their past and carried unhealed wounds within their own psyche. They, too, lived in a culture that did not support their essential nature. Our parents could not give us what they did not have, and they could not help but pass some of their own wounding onto us. Even the most well-meaning parents cannot give their children the essential support they are unable to experience within themselves.

In order to survive we unknowingly abandoned our essential self and followed the instructions provided by our caregivers and by the world around us. In a multiplicity of ways we were taught not to trust our own essential nature. We learned to rely upon the outside world, not only for our survival but also for our identity itself.

We learned to be the child that our parents wanted us to be so that we could get what we needed. We were rewarded for some behaviors and not rewarded, or punished, for others. This may have been overt and obvious or it may have been very subtle; it may have been verbal or nonverbal, but at a very young age we learned the meaning of "good" and "bad" as well as the consequences of each.

Getting what we needed by being "good" gave us satisfaction and pleasure. Not getting what we needed—being "bad"—resulted in dissatisfaction and pain. When a particular (good) behavior is met with the experience of pleasure, we will repeat it over and over again. If a (bad) behavior is met with the experience of pain, we will cease the behavior. As this occurs many times, we eventually repress *even the impulse or desire* for this (bad) behavior. Not only do we judge the behavior to be bad, but even the impulse or desire for such behavior is deemed to be bad. Eventually we dismiss it completely from awareness.

We developed habituated patterns of thinking and behavior that produced pleasure by getting what we needed. And we developed habituated patterns of thinking and behavior that avoided the pain of being punished or ignored. As we developed a sense of self separate from mother, our sense of self began to coalesce around these habit patterns. Our habituated strategies became the core of our identity.

The essential nature is natural, spontaneous and free. It cannot function freely when it is restricted by habituated patterns and repressed desires. As our sense of self became identified with the habituated personality patterns, we experienced separation from our essential nature. This false self feels a sense of emptiness at its very core. We survived; but we paid a price. The price we paid was to acquire an identity that is disconnected from essential nature and feels empty at its core.

A primary intention of the false self is to avoid feeling this sense of emptiness, this pain of separation. Fear of this core emptiness drives the life of every false self. Anything that threatens this ego façade touches our fear of this core emptiness. The false self has a vested interest in not being exposed; it attempts to masquerade as our true self.

The ego is like an operating system in a computer—it is very powerful because it manages what is presented, and how it's presented to our conscious awareness; this is all determined by our core beliefs. The ego system not only interprets our perceptions but also determines *which* perceptions will even *come into conscious awareness*. Once the core belief system is established, this system will amplify and embellish those perceptions that reinforce the core beliefs and tend to filter out those that seem to contradict it. The ego behaves like a living entity with its own drive and strategy for survival.

Every ego has a set of core beliefs that structures its search for external fulfillment and its attempt to protect itself from feeling its own core emptiness. These are actually more than beliefs alone; they are beliefs embedded in a collection of memories, emotions and physical sensations.

This ego system rests upon the beliefs of who we are, who we should be, and what we need to do to get our needs met. Most of these beliefs are not true, but they did help us to survive and to function in our family of origin. They must have worked in some way; otherwise we would not have kept them.

This belief system becomes problematic when we embrace it as a universal truth. Assuming our beliefs to be reality, we unwittingly use them to function as an adult, after we leave our family of origin. We use these beliefs as a lens through which we see the world, forgetting that it was simply a strategy that we adopted to survive as a child. We eventually find that this does not work. We discover that we are no longer children, that the world is not like our family, and what we thought to be universally true, isn't.

Repression and the Shadow

Very early in life we learned the advantages of being the child our parents wanted us to be. This self that we wanted to show our parents, and eventually, the world, became a mask that we habitually wore; in time we identified with it—it became our sense of self. Jung called this our *persona*, which means *mask*. This is the false self that we have come to believe is real.

Any desires, impulses and emotions that threatened the façade of the persona were eventually repressed into the unconscious. Beneath our conscious awareness lies a reservoir of unexpressed impulses, desires and emotions held at bay by the ego structure. This collection of repressed energies eventually coalesces into an underground subpersonality, which Jung called the *shadow*.

The shadow is a collection of parts of our self that have been deemed bad, inferior or dangerous, first by our parents, and then by ourselves. These qualities seemed so bad that we eventually refused to believe that they ever were a part of us. The shadow is the psychological equivalent of a leper colony: it houses the sick and ugly parts of our self that we have driven into exile so that we do not have to look at them. The shadow is hidden from view; it is not directly accessible to conscious awareness. We may readily see these qualities in others, but definitely not in ourselves!

The contents of the shadow are not inherently evil or sick. They may appear that way because we have been taught to see them as such. And they may appear sick or evil because they have been neglected and unloved. Any child who is neglected and unloved will be psychologically sick and may express problematic behavior; but no child—or any part of our self—is inherently bad.

We consciously identify with the persona; we unconsciously identify with the shadow. We may consciously identify our self as a nice, pleasant, agreeable individual, but unconsciously be identified with quite the opposite—an angry, argumentative and domineering curmudgeon. We do our best to hide this shadow, but it never stays completely submerged; it constantly seeks opportunities to emerge.

In the ego identification, we live in a constant state of internal conflict. Symptoms of this conflict can appear in many forms: insecurity, worry, stress, depression and so on. Like a fugitive from the law, we fear being discovered, not so much by others as by ourselves. We are both the fugitive and the cop, engaged in a perpetual drama of self-deception and hiding.

The ego is constantly at war with itself. But even the acknowledgement of this war can be a threat to the ego's façade of control, so it will disown even the symptoms of repression. It tries to hide the symptoms of the shadow as well as the shadow itself. The ego is like a corrupt dictator who not only imprisons dissidents but denies the existence of any such imprisonment.

Living at war with our self diminishes the fullest expression of our potential. Our body can become a casualty of this war, and it may be affected in many ways: stress-related illness, chronic tension, fatigue, depression, anxiety and many other symptoms. We can never be a whole person when we are at war with our self. At best, we live only half of our life.

If we repress anger, then we have denied much of our power and vitality. We have deprived ourselves of learning the healthy expression of anger and the ability to transform this energy into ways that can effect positive changes in our world. Beneath all anger lies an unmet need. Refusal to acknowledge anger may block the recognition and the fulfillment of that need. Anger is part of the grieving process; it is a stage in our healing. Failure to acknowledge anger can result in lingering depression, which is often symptomatic of unfulfilled desires and unfelt grief.

If we repress our sexuality, we diminish the ability to experience pleasure in all areas of our life. Since creativity is related to sexual energy, if we repress our sexuality then we have denied much of our creative energy as well. Our sexuality is closely related to our primal life energy; to be fully alive, we must acknowledge our sexuality and be willing to address and to heal our sexual wounds.

If we repress our vulnerability, then we have closed our heart to life; to be truly alive is to be vulnerable. Caring and compassion can arise only from our willingness to be open and vulnerable. If we are perpetually armored against being hurt, it is virtually impossible to have an intimate relationship with anyone—including our self.

Fear and shame are the primary forces that keep the shadow submerged. The shadow stays hidden because of fear: the fear of acknowledging that which seems too dangerous, too painful or too shameful. Our fears may become projected onto our environment so that we become afraid of rejection, failure or abuse. But what we really fear has already happened: conscious awareness of the memories, emotions and pain that we are holding inside us. To become whole and to consciously evolve, we must acknowledge and embrace all aspects of our self.

Embracing all aspects of self does not necessarily mean acting them out. We may be holding desires and emotions that could be harmful or destructive if we acted from them. We must acknowledge and embrace these energies internally, talk about them in an appropriate setting but not act them out on anyone. We can develop the skills to discharge these energies in ways that are not violent or harmful to anyone. This may require getting help from a professional counselor, coach or psychotherapist.

The Irony of Addiction

The shadow lives in constant fear of being exposed and is deeply ashamed of who it believes itself to be. It is very painful to live this way. Some turn to addiction or compulsive behavior as an attempt to escape this pain.

Substance abuse and addictive behavior are symptoms of the shadow and its denied pain. Addiction begins as an attempt to obtain relief from pain and anxiety, as well as to experience a state of euphoria. It temporarily achieves this but with a very high price tag: The suffering we seek to avoid still remains, but we have now added another layer of suffering on top of it, which results from the addiction and its consequences.

What all of us most want is the experience of our own essential nature. This yearning is behind every worldly desire. When we are out of contact with our own essence, we look for our fulfillment from the world. To fulfill our desires, we develop a strategy that requires repressing some aspect of our self, because that quality appears to be a threat to the fulfillment of our desires.

In repressing that aspect of our self, we are further disconnecting our contact with essence. In doing this we are actually moving away from that which we desire the most—our own true nature. This disconnection creates a painful sense of deficiency that propels us even more strongly toward external fulfillment. This cycle is the engine that drives all addiction.

The more we seek external fulfillment, the further we move from our true nature, which is present here and now. The further we move away from true nature, the more anxiety we experience. To avoid this anxiety, we become ever more entrenched in our addiction.

Recovery from addiction requires modifying our behavior to abstain from the addiction. But this alone is not enough; we must see the cycle that drives the addiction. We must face and embrace that which we have been running from by indulging in the addiction. It requires new understandings and new choices. Recovery is much more than abstinence; it is recovering the lost self hidden by the addiction.

Repression and Relationships

Our ego strategies have become our identity. The ego is disconnected from essential nature and feels empty at its core. Fear of facing this core emptiness is the driving energy of every ego. Some of us will seek an intimate relationship as an attempt to avoid the emptiness, but it doesn't work. Like any addiction, it ultimately takes us further from that which we are truly seeking, which is our own essential nature.

Sally came to me for counseling with the complaint of having many failed relationships. She said that she tried everything in her power to be the kind of person her partner wanted her to be; but she ended up feeling unappreciated and never received the attention that she wanted from her partner.

After some exploration, Sally told me that her parents wanted her to be what she describes as "Little Miss Sunshine." She grew up believing that only if she was sweet and pretty, and put everyone else first, could she get the attention and affection of her parents. The few times that she ever expressed anger, or formed her own power, she was told that "this is not the good little girl that mommy and daddy wanted."

Before long, Sally began to live out their expectations. It had many rewards, but it was also quite difficult. Sally never found her own voice or a sense of personal power. As an adult she learned to get what she wanted by pleasing others and by "being nice," but it never seemed to be enough for her partners. They became tired of her constant demand for attention; and they often said that they wanted her to be "more real." She could not understand what they meant by this.

Sally created a strategy of becoming the "Little Miss Sunshine" that she believed her parents wanted her to be. It apparently worked for her as a child, so she began to identify with this strategy. She did not see it as a strategy—it just seemed to be "herself." As an adult, she could not understand why this did not work in her intimate relationships as it did in her family. Sally was working from a map that was out of date and no longer useful.

To recover contact with her essential nature, Sally must first see how she still uses this strategy to get what she wants. It might be helpful for her to explore her early relationship with her parents to see how this pattern was used. Sally must be willing to let go of this strategy to discover what is beneath it. Above all, she must be willing to face the anxiety and pain that she tried to avoid as a child by adopting this persona.

Sally must be willing to face the feelings of deficiency that arise when a child's needs are not met. As a child this seemed far too painful, but as an adult she has the capacity to face this. Along the way, she may encounter some buried anger. This emotion was problematic in childhood, but if, as an adult, she learns to handle it skillfully, then it can empower her to get her needs met in a healthy way.

Sally repressed her anger because she believed that her parents would abandon her if she expressed it. When she approaches her experience of anger, Sally will likely experience fear of that abandonment. Before she can directly address the anger, she may have to work with the fear and sorrow that arises from her feelings of abandonment. A part of Sally *was* actually abandoned by her parents—a part that they could not acknowledge within themselves, such as their own anger.

Underneath all of this lies her essential nature, which has remained hidden and undeveloped beneath her ego strategies. As Sally begins to discover within herself what she has been seeking from others, the strategies will begin to dissolve and she will develop healthier relationships. She will begin to relate to others as a healthy adult rather than as a wounded child. As she expresses her own essential nature, she will become more attractive to others and will find deeper intimacy in all her relationships. But most important, Sally will discover the treasure that she is and always was.

Projection

A primary symptom of the shadow lies in the phenomenon of *projection*: That which we refuse to see within our self will appear to be present in our environment—usually in another person. This phenomenon is aptly named because it does function much like a movie projector—what we cannot see "behind" us appears to exist out in front of us. Any unconscious aspect of the psyche is like an image on a filmstrip; when it is projected, it appears to be outside of us and much larger that it really is. What we refuse to see internally, we will see externally.

Our world is like a stage upon which our "internal players" act out their roles following a script that we ourselves have written. The world reveals our self to us: What we don't see in the shadows is shown to us in broad daylight. The meanings that we ascribe to people and events in our life correspond to a script written long ago. But if we are not conscious, we will believe our projected meaning to be reality; we will believe it to be an accurate perception of some person or circumstance in our life.

Projection causes us to live with a distorted view of reality; it creates a world of illusion. We are not seeing the world as it is; we are seeing it as we are. Jung wrote: "Projections change the world into the replica of one's own unknown face."[33]

If we are unconscious of an aspect of our psyche, it will appear to be in others, perhaps magnified. It appears to be 100 percent within them and zero percent within us. We may loathe, or long for, a trait that we see in others, believing our self to be totally devoid of this quality.

We may find ourselves "fatally attracted" to someone in spite of all common sense, or we may become enraged at another person for very little reason. We may habitually find fault with someone and secretly want to punish them for their "shameful" behavior. We may have an undue and unquestioning admiration for someone or be inordinately fearful of some authority figure. All of these are examples of projection. That which we cannot see within will seem to appear in our environment.

Public figures, such as politicians, movie actors or TV personalities are typical targets for projection. When Princess Grace died, millions of people around the world who never met her mourned her death as if she was a member of their own family. Our entertainment media thrives on the phenomenon of projection. At the time of this writing, one of our most popular TV shows is named *American Idol*.

Conversely, we have historically belittled or condemned certain groups or types of people: women, minorities, foreigners, criminals and persons with disabilities have long been targets for projection, sometimes with dire consequences.

Although the term *shadow* usually implies a negative aspect of the psyche, for simplicity I am using the term to include both the positive and negative aspects of self that are hidden from our view. We may be projecting a "dark shadow" or a "bright shadow." In either case, we see a trait in someone else that we believe is not in ourselves. It appears to be "all about them, and not about me!"

When we discover that we are projecting onto another person, it does not necessarily mean that they are devoid of the particular trait that we perceive. It may be that they *do* have the characteristic that we see so clearly. *But so what?* What is that to me? When we are projecting, we don't just perceive something, we create a story about what we are seeing, and typically it's a story where *we* are omniscient and pure, and the other person deserves eternal damnation.

Not every time we feel fear, anger or admiration for someone are we projecting onto them. But when that feeling is unusually strong or persistent, then it is very possibly a projection, especially if this feeling recurs frequently. Any inordinate attraction, admiration, fear or condemnation of someone or something is usually indicative of projection.

Relationship and Projection

Projection is usually involved in any relationship problem. The human drama is one of living out our internal world through our relationship with others. If we stay awake, we can use these experiences to reclaim lost parts of our self. If we are not awake, then we simply propagate suffering in our life and in our world.

Our intimate relationships, particularly the romantic ones, are vehicles through which the shadow is projected. When someone triggers an unconscious facet of our psyche then projection is activated. Falling in love is itself a projection; we can fall in love with someone we barely know! And this is why, after we get to really know our beloved, we may become disillusioned, because the person we've fallen in love with never really existed in the first place. The bubble of fantasy has burst and reality stares us in the face. Then the real work of loving another person begins.

Contrary to many song lyrics, no other person can fulfill all of our desires and bring us eternal happiness. However, an intimate relationship can become a powerful vehicle for healing and awakening. Such a relationship can be a powerful mirror for discovering aspects of self not possible when being alone. It can reveal places within us that need to be healed. Our partner can be our teacher if we are open to self-discovery rather than self-justification.

Ron and Sarah came to me for counseling. They had been married about two years and the honeymoon was definitely over!

Sarah complained that she could not get the time and attention that she wanted from Ron and that he always seemed to be preoccupied. She said that he was constantly critical of her, which made her feel as though she couldn't do anything right. Sarah was attracted to Ron because she liked his strength and stability, but that was no longer enough for her.

Ron, in turn, complained that Sarah would never leave him alone. She constantly demanded his time and attention. He felt burdened by the relationship. He said that he loved Sarah very much but needed more of his own space. He was attracted to his wife because of her wonderful caring heart, and he liked the attention she gave him. However, he noted that the tension had been building for several months, and "too much of a good thing is not a good thing."

Ron and Sarah were calling forth repressed aspects of one another's psyche. Ron grew up believing that he had to do everything just right to acquire his parents' love and attention. He was severely criticized for his mistakes. He developed an ego structure based upon the strategy of never making a mistake. To give Sarah the time and attention she wanted meant letting go of his constant busyness and his striving for perfection. He confided that he secretly felt that if he fully opened his heart to Sarah, his deepest flaws would be revealed. This was very threatening to his ego ideal.

Sarah grew up being the emotional caretaker for her father. Her mother had a chronic illness so her father got most of his emotional support from Sarah, his oldest daughter. Because she was responsible for her father's emotional well-being, her ego strategy formed around this belief. She felt that if she gave up trying to make Ron happy she would lose him; then she would have no reason for living. Sarah felt much anxiety when Ron did not depend upon her as her father did.

For both of them, their resistance to facing the shadow was threatening their relationship. Once they saw this, they were eventually willing to face their worst fears, because they each loved one another and did not want the relationship to end. It is highly unlikely they would have had the opportunity or the incentive to engage in this very challenging inner work if they were not in a committed relationship. Relationship can be a catalyst for healing the shadow.

On the other hand, *not* being in a relationship can be a catalyst for others.

Janet told me that she had been in a relationship "almost as far back as I can remember." As an adult she never went more than a few months without becoming involved with someone. She came to see me after her third divorce. Dating a man named Bill, Janet was about to enter into another committed relationship. She was not really in love with Bill, but she was afraid to be alone, and this was "better than being alone." She came to see me because she suspected that she was running away from herself by jumping into yet another relationship.

As we explored her past, she shared with me that her father died suddenly when she was only 3 years old. She does not remember any details but does remember missing him terribly. She also recalls some family members telling her that she had to be a big girl because Mommy needed her. She has no recollection of openly grieving her loss.

After a few sessions, Janet began to see the connection between her unresolved grief and her fear of being alone. Not having a man in her life reminded her of growing up without the father that she needed. She began to see how this fear caused her to jump into unhealthy relationships—often against her better judgment.

Her work was to begin grieving the loss of her father. She would grieve his loss not just as a 40-year-old woman, but also as a 3-year-old child. It was not easy, but as she opened her heart to her childhood grief she began to heal. Over time, Janet became more comfortable being alone and became more discerning in her committed relationships.

From these brief stories we can see the power of relationship to uncover shadow issues and to provide the incentive for deep healing. To truly love another, we must be willing to love all aspects of our self, especially those that have been hidden from our view. The most loving thing that we can do for anyone—partner, child or friend—is to love all the elements of our self.

Knowing that what we truly desire is our own essential self, we cease to see others as objects to fill our deficiencies. When we don't need something from another person, we can see him or her as they really are, rather than as an object to fill our needs. We will begin to experience a natural compassion for others as well as for ourselves. Our relationships will become more fulfilling—for ourselves, and for others as well.

What we really want from others can be found only within our self. When we cease trying to get happiness from others, and when are willing to accept our feelings of deficiency with compassion, we will eventually discover that what we truly seek is always within our self. Everything that we truly need, we already are.

In Summary

1. To evolve beyond our current level, we must understand how we became involved in it. Involution reoccurs with the birth of every living being. You are Spirit calling itself *me*.

2. At a very early age we create internal maps to support our survival, to make sense of our world, and to give us a sense of control over our life. The foundation of all these maps is a map called *me* — the ego.

3. And who is this me, really? This question cannot be satisfactorily answered with words. But the mind is not content with not knowing, so it identifies the self in the only way it knows how: by describing the self in contrast to all that is around it.

4. The teachings of ancient wisdom tell us that who we really are exists in a realm *beyond* time and space. But mind can only function *within* time and space. So there is a huge hole in ego's ability to know itself. The ego sees this hole as an emptiness as frightening as death itself.

5. To become free of the false self, it is important to see how we became entrapped in it and how we continue to entrap ourselves. The false self is not an object; it is a pattern of habituated thoughts, feelings and behaviors.

6. We use the term *personality* to denote the psychic structure of the individual person. The personality becomes the false self when we believe that it is real and all of who we are. When we awaken to our true nature, the personality does not cease to exist; it becomes transparent to essence.

7. We are born with few instincts to survive in the physical world. We learn how to survive primarily from our family. As a child's needs are met through the quality of essence in the parent, the child learns to rely upon his own essential nature. But usually our needs were not met in this manner, so we learned to not trust our own essential nature and to follow instructions provided by the world.

8. We developed patterns of behavior that produced the desired results. Our identity coalesced around these patterns. This identity exists without awareness of essential nature; it feels empty at its core. The ego continuously seeks to avoid this feeling of emptiness.

9. The ego has a core belief system focused on external fulfill-ment. This core belief system is the foundation of our sense of self. This belief system is very powerful because it manages what is presented to conscious awareness as well as how it is presented.

10. We formed a self that is what we thought our parents wanted us to be. Jung called this the *persona*. All that did not conform to the persona was repressed into the unconscious and formed the *shadow*. We usually see the shadow as dangerous and infe-rior, but this only appears true—in reality it is not.

11. The ego identity is constantly at war with itself. This causes many problems. We can never be a whole person when we are at war with ourselves; we live a greatly diminished life.

12. Fear and shame keep the shadow submerged. To embrace these and other aspects of the shadow does not necessarily mean to act them out.

13. One symptom of the shadow is addiction. Addiction drives us further from our essential nature. Recovery involves willing-ness to face our hidden pain.

14. Relationships can be a means of discovering and healing the shadow. Intimate relationships often uncover our hidden pain and may provide the incentive for facing and healing this pain.

15. We project the shadow by refusing to believe these shadow qualities exist within us; instead, we see it in others. This gives us a distorted view of reality. Inordinate fear and/or judgment may be signs of projection.

16. All that we seek is ultimately within ourselves; it is our own essential nature. If we cease trying to find fulfillment in the world and look within, we will eventually find what we most desire. The journey is never easy, but the life that opens to us is worth the struggle—many times over.

Segue

In this chapter we have explored the experience of involution; that is Spirit losing itself in human form and falling asleep. We looked at the symptoms of this sleep and the reasons to awaken. To awaken is to evolve. In the remaining chapters, we look at this experience of evolution, which is Spirit awakening to Itself.

4

Embracing Our Wholeness

In the 1960s, the United States received a gift from another country, which was a rare and beautiful white tiger named Mohini. For years, Mohini lived in the Washington, D.C., National Zoo, spending her days pacing back and forth in a 12-by 12-foot cage, continuously walking the same figure-eight pattern hundreds of times a day ... every single day.

After many years, zoo officials decided to build her a much larger habitat, which would include several acres of trees, grassy hills and a pond. In this lush environment Mohini would be able to run, climb and explore. But when she arrived at her spacious new home, Mohini did not respond the way they had expected. She did not rush out to eagerly explore what would seem to be her natural habitat. Instead, she immediately ran to a far corner of the compound, near a wall, and began pacing back and forth within an area 12- by 12-foot square. She paced that same figure-eight pattern until the grass was worn bare. She continued this behavior until the day she died.

Most of us are saddened by such a story, perhaps because we might in some way identify with Mohini. The tiger is a symbol of wildness, freedom, power and beauty; these are all qualities of our own essential nature, present within each of us. It seems tragic enough when this natural aliveness is blocked by external circumstances, such as the original cage that housed Mohini. But the level of tragedy feels even greater when the external cage has become internalized and keeps one a prisoner long after the original bars have been removed. The bars still exist, but only in the mind.

Like Mohini, we each found a way to cope with the limitations imposed upon us. We developed certain habituated mental patterns that dulled the pain that arises when our essential nature is stifled. We survived by mechanically conforming, living less than the fullness of our life. At the time, this may seem like our only alternative.

Yet our very feeling of sadness is evidence that we are still alive. Returning to greater aliveness begins with awareness of what we feel. Indeed, awareness of our present moment experience is always the first step in awakening to our essential nature.

Let us indulge in a thought experiment. Imagine that we hired a "tiger therapist" to help Mohini break free from her mechanized routine and live a fuller life in her new environment. This hypothetical therapist might begin by asking Mohini about her present moment experience: "What are you aware of? What are you feeling right now?" The therapist would ask Mohini if she is aware that she is no longer in the same cage and that the bars are no longer there.

If and when Mohini could see her present reality, then the therapist might point out that she has a choice to make: She can continue her routine and feel safe or choose to live differently and be more alive and free, but the price of freedom would not be small.

Mohini would need to face her feelings about having had her wild nature crushed by being forced to live in a small cage for so many years. She would likely discover a great deal of rage. That energy would have to be discharged safely—lots of roaring would ensue! Eventually she would feel intense grief resulting from her lost freedom. And then, Mohini would need to learn how to function in a completely new way in her new environment. Recovery would not be an easy process, but certainly possible if she had the will and the courage.

This fantasy illustrates some of the stages of healing. It's not easy, but each step along the way Mohini is becoming more alive and free. To avoid the discomfort would be to avoid the healing. Perhaps Mohini did not have the ability to make the choice for healing; we do.

No matter what our past choices have been, we can make a new one right now. We can and do always choose the meaning that we are giving to the present moment's experience. We can do this consciously or unconsciously. Only if we do it consciously can we make new choices and find new ways to understand our life experiences. We can choose to reclaim our lost essence. This is always possible because our essential nature is never lost. However, it can be hidden, and sometimes it is buried quite deep.

To heal is to release illusions that we have embraced as truth. We may have held these thinking-feeling patterns for a long time. If they are to come out, it must be in the same way they went in: through the gate of awareness. As these patterns were formed, we believed that they reflected reality. As they come out for healing, they can feel very real at times. This is why it is *so* important to stay present each moment. Otherwise we will be seduced by the old patterns. They will become our reality ... for a while.

The power of our intention to heal will not allow us to remain lost for long. It is inevitable that we will get lost, at first, but as we persist, we find that our lapses gradually decrease in frequency and duration.

It is important to return our focus to our highest truth as we engage this process. We may need help from others to do this; this is the function of the teacher, the counselor, the support system and so on. We may need someone to hold that truth for us when we have temporarily forgotten. Our support system can remind us that anytime we become more conscious, we are evolving. Evolution is always in the direction of greater awareness.

Reclaiming the Shadow

Our evolutionary task at this juncture is to reclaim our essential nature. We begin by reclaiming the lost parts of the personality. We have been referring to these lost parts as the *shadow*. Our work is to integrate the shadow into conscious awareness. The shadow is, in reality, our essential nature in disguise. It is disguised because we have rejected it; we have refused to see it as it truly is. Instead, we see it in the way that we originally responded to it: with fear, with shame, with judgment. *The shadow is a mirror of our own conscious attitude toward it*. If we fear it, it will appear frightening; if we despise it, it will appear shameful; if we reject it, it will haunt us until we accept it.

But rather than seeing it as a reflection of our own attitude, we often see it as an objective reality. A story from India tells of a great artist who painted a large picture of a tiger on the inside wall of his home. He painted it so lifelike that he became afraid to enter his own house! Such is our relationship to the shadow.

If we can befriend the shadow, it will become a good friend and a trusted ally. There are many ways to reclaim the shadow and to transform it from adversary to ally. One way is to become aware of projections as they fire up in our everyday experiences. To review and summarize what we presented earlier, here are some symptoms of projection:

- An emotional response, positive or negative, that seems out of proportion to circumstances and disproportionate in intensity or duration.

- A lingering and chronic emotional reaction to a given person or circumstance.

- Obsessive emotions or desires—positive or negative—toward anyone or anything.

Once you become aware that you are projecting, then become conscious of your thoughts and emotions. Pay attention to self-talk and to internal dialogue; see if you can determine the particular belief that is fueling the emotion. This is not self-analysis; it is a process of direct awareness. Avoid the familiar tendency to ask, "*Why* am I feeling like this?" This question usually gets us nowhere. Simply ask: "What am I feeling right now? What am I telling myself? What do I want? What do I experience in my body at this time?" Allow yourself to experience all of your feelings fully.

We are not looking for some supposed "cause" to what we are thinking or feeling, and we are not looking at what we "should be" thinking or feeling; we simply look at what is present *right now* as objectively as possible.

Just to know that we are projecting and be willing to use this experience for healing is a huge step. Awareness and self-responsibility is the key. Self-responsibility is not blaming oneself; it is simply acknowledging the true source of our unhappiness. The source of our unhappiness is always within our self. Circumstances and other people can be a trigger or catalyst for our difficulty, but *our response* to any experience is always *our responsibility*.

Not every emotion that we experience is a symptom of the shadow or of projection. Emotions are natural responses to some life experiences. In shadow work, we are looking for chronic, overly intense or unhealthy expressions of our emotions.

The term *shadow*, as it was originally coined by Jung, refers to repression of despised aspects of the psyche: those that act in opposition to the conscious intentions of the persona. Jung perceived that other psychic energies, besides the shadow, are unconscious and can be projected. He referred to these energies as *archetypes* and *complexes*.[34] For the sake of simplicity I will not address these aspects of the psyche individually but will include them under the general term *shadow*. The process for integrating these unconscious patterns is essentially the same as that for the shadow.

To begin our discussion, it is helpful to see that before we discover the shadow itself, we will experience the *shadow symptom*. The symptom is actually a defensive posture taken to protect us from experiencing the shadow directly. The symptom is the conscious attitude that we have toward the shadow content itself. We may be secretly ashamed or afraid of the quality held in the shadow. We typically experience this same attitude toward others when they openly express a quality that is reflected in our own shadow.

As an example, let's say that someone is openly expressing sadness, and we find ourselves critically judging this person for exhibiting sadness. Perhaps we want to tell her to "get over it," or we may judge him as a "crybaby." This judgment reflects the attitude that we are secretly holding toward our own repressed sadness. The attitude we have toward the other person is a reflection of the attitude we are holding towards this aspect of our self. This is the shadow symptom.

If we find our self feeling judgmental or unduly afraid of someone who exhibits aggressiveness or anger, for example, then it is likely that we secretly fear our own anger that we carry in the shadow. (This assumes that we are not physically threatened by this person; in which case, fear would be a natural response.)

Why would we be ashamed or afraid of these parts of our self? The answer is that we were taught to do so. It is possible that we were shamed or threatened when we exhibited this emotion, so we eventually learned to do it to our self internally. Or it may be that this particular emotion was taboo in our family system, so the threat was implicit rather than explicit. By implication: "If you

want to be part of this family, then you will not do thus-and-so."
Repression became a way of protecting our self from some antic-
ipated punishment or attack; we internalized our caregivers in an
attempt to protect ourselves—originally from the caregivers
themselves, and later from our own projections.[35]

If we find our self obsessively attracted to someone, then we
may be projecting a part of our essential nature onto that person.
As we were not supported to directly discover our essential
nature, we may have been taught that this essential quality lies
outside of us. We may see someone else having it and believe that
we lack it completely, and that we need this other person in order
to (vicariously) experience it. We can worship saints and avatars
because we are projecting our disowned essential nature onto
them, believing that they carry for us what we ourselves are lacking. We may project an essential quality onto some role, position
or title that we believe will provide us with the quality presumed
lacking within our self.

We may become addicted to some substance or behavior
because it induces an experience that mimics the experience of
our own essential nature. Certain drugs and behaviors give us the
experience of being "high." It was Jung who first recognized alco-
holism as a spiritual disease. He saw that for the addict, the "spirits" in the bottle provided a counterfeit experience of one's own
Spirit, and that only by opening to our own Spirit, our Higher
Power, can we effectively confront the disease.

Dialoguing With the Shadow

Another way of reclaiming the shadow is to begin *dialoguing*
with it. This dialogue can take two primary forms. One form is
that of journal writing. In journal writing, we allow the hidden
parts of our self to "speak" to us through the written word. We
call upon this hidden part to "talk" to us as if it were another person. It is as if the conscious mind is engaging in a dialogue with

some aspect of the unconscious through the medium of writing.[36] Record in the journal your own (conscious) "voice" as well as the "voice" of the shadow as you inwardly hear it respond to you.

For example, let us say that you are chronically critical of a particular person and these harsh judgments seem out of proportion to circumstances, so you suspect that projection is at work. Given that, you then begin by accepting the fact that your reaction is, in reality, toward some part of yourself and not the other person. Even if he or she is acting badly, your response is *your* responsibility, not theirs. And, upon acknowledging this, it is very important to abstain from self-judgment; you are not "bad" because you are projecting.

So we begin our work by dialoguing with the shadow symptom. The shadow symptom is our immediate response to what we perceive in another. We see that the shadow symptom is judgment that arises in response to something seen in another. Let's call this symptom the *Judge*. The Judge sees something in this other person that you don't want to see in yourself. The job of the Judge is to maintain this repression by helping you believe that your response is justified because what you see in them is *absolutely* "bad" or "wrong" and that this quality is totally within them and not at all within yourself.

In the dialogue process, you ask the Judge to internally speak to you, and then you listen quietly. Write down the words that you hear in your mind. After the Judge is finished speaking, you can respond in writing. Thus a dialogue ensues. Continue the process as long as you sense the Judge speaking. Do not edit, judge or analyze what you hear. Let it be spontaneous and intuitive. Be open and accepting of all the memories and emotions that arise; record these as well. You may record your dialogues over several sessions and periodically review them to see how things progress. Generally, the longer one works with this process, the easier it will become.

After dialoguing with the shadow symptom, you may begin to feel the shadow characteristic itself arising. The shadow characteristic is the quality that you see in the other person that reflects what is repressed within your unconscious. Typically the shadow characteristic is something that makes you feel very vulnerable and is quite unpleasant. This is why it was repressed—because it did not feel safe to own it as part of yourself.

Let's say that the quality you discover behind the Judge is *shame*. You saw someone do something that you would never do because it is "so shameful." Now you begin to see that the shame is not in the other person or in what they did, but it is hidden within yourself. Perhaps you were shamed when you did this thing, therefore you deemed the act itself as shameful and you deemed yourself shameful for wanting to do it; repressed into the unconscious, it comes out via projection onto another.

Dialogue with this quality as you become aware of it; dialogue with the shame itself. Let it have a voice; respond to it. Record the internal voices in your journal. Continue the process, working with whatever feelings or memories that arise. Stay present to the process; avoid editing, judging or analyzing anything that you experience. Always be gentle and patient with yourself.

Another way to engage this process is to give these parts of you an actual, objective voice. For example, you could "let the Judge speak." It is very important that you speak as if you *were* the Judge; you speak *from* this voice, not *about* it. Experience the energy of the Judge as you speak from it. Then return to "yourself" and respond as your normal self. You can do this into a voice recorder and then listen back when your session is over. Or, you can do this with a coach or a guide. If you do, it's best to use someone who has some training and experience with this process.[37]

The first step is to recognize projection: to be able to identify it when, or as soon as possible, after it has occurred. The second step is to work with the shadow symptom in the form of written or vocal dialogue. The third step is to dialogue with the shadow characteristic itself. The final step is to fully, directly and consciously experience the emotion or quality that is being projected. (A reminder: Accepting a feeling does not mean acting it out or believing it's an objective truth.) Feel the emotions that arise; feel the sensations in your body. Be aware of any thoughts or memories that appear as you do this. Accept what appears without judgment. If self-judgment does appear, then just notice it but do not react to it, and do not believe it. Once again, always be gentle and patient with yourself.

When we work with the shadow symptom and consciously embrace it, we find the shadow characteristic itself, which is a more vulnerable or intense feeling beneath the symptom. In our example, we worked with the Judge and eventually embraced that aspect, and then we saw shame as the shadow characteristic itself. We can see that the Judge was actually trying to protect us from feeling the pain of the shame. And beneath the shame may lie a deeper wound, perhaps a feeling of abandonment, betrayal or loss.

Be patient and accepting of whatever arises, and continue the work as long as needed. It is not helpful to think in terms of trying to "get rid" of something or to "work through it and get over it." This attitude is not conducive to healing.

The healing of the shadow occurs when we:

- Recognize the symptoms of projection.
- Consciously experience these symptoms and fully accept them.
- Dialogue with the symptoms.
- Work with deeper feelings that emerge; this may be the shadow characteristic itself.
- Dialogue with the shadow characteristic.

- Consciously experience and embrace this quality within yourself; allow the full experience of the feelings that arise.
- Cultivate understanding and compassion for why this quality was initially repressed into the shadow; be patient and gentle with yourself.

Subpersonalities

The unconscious is not a homogenous psychic mass. It is a conglomerate, a collection of various subpersonalities. Some of these subpersonalities are interrelated and some are totally unaware of one another. These subpersonalities generally reside in the unconscious, but events and conditions in our life can bring one or more of them into conscious awareness. They are like a cast of characters standing in the wings awaiting their cue to go onstage.

When they do come "onstage," they typically occupy all of our attention: We are totally identified with them. And these "little people" can jump out and grab us at the most inopportune times! If we walk past a doughnut shop, one subpersonality may jump out and convince us that we absolutely deserve a fresh, hot doughnut and that life will be incomplete if we miss this opportunity. If we give in and indulge this desire, a few minutes later another subpersonality may emerge scolding us unmercifully for being weak and indulgent. It can make us wonder who we really are.

The following poem expresses this quandary:

Within this temple there's a crowd.
There's one of us who's humble,
And one who's proud;
One who is sorry for his sins;

Another, unrepentant, sits and grins;
From much earthly care I could be free
If I could just determine
Which is me.
—Anonymous

A subpersonality is a collection of habituated beliefs, emotions and behaviors that were formed to meet a specific need in our life.[38] Together they form our various ego strategies.

We are unconsciously identified with a subpersonality until we bring it into conscious awareness. When it is unconscious, it can control our life—sometimes as if another person were inside of us. It wasn't the devil that made you do it, it was a subpersonality that hijacked your conscious awareness and took it over!

Integrating these subpersonalities into conscious awareness is similar to that of shadow work. When they are integrated, we will have conscious access to them and can use them in ways that serve us better; thus we have transformed the subpersonality from an adversary into an ally.

The integration process is also similar to that of working with projection. The first step is to become aware of the subpersonality as soon as possible after it takes over. Become aware of the particular thoughts, emotions and behaviors that arise as this subpersonality emerges.

Let's say you have a subpersonality that always says "yes" when you really want to say "no." You may find yourself agreeing to do things that you later regret. You may become angry with yourself afterwards for giving in to something that you don't really want to do.

Become aware of the circumstances that trigger this subpersonality. If someone asks you to do something for them, the first thing to do is take a deep breath and decide if you truly want to do this. Interrupt the habituated response of saying "yes." You may need to tell the other person that you will let them know later. This will allow you to have time to consider your choice. Give yourself permission to do it differently.

When you can, let yourself feel the energy of the subpersonality that immediately wants to say "yes." Close your eyes and ask this subpersonality to present itself to you as an *image*. What does he, she, it look like? How old is she? Get acquainted with her. Dialogue with her; ask her questions: What purpose do you serve? What do you need? What gift do you have for me?

This subpersonality was formed in the past to meet a specific need; to help you get what you want. Determine what that need is. Perhaps there is a better way to get this need met in your current life circumstance. Do some journal writing or vocal dialogue with the subpersonality.

Look at the self-talk and feelings that arise when you break with your habituated response. Perhaps fear of rejection arises; maybe an internal critic arises scolding you for being selfish. If so, then see that this is just another subpersonality emerging. See how this subpersonality may have developed to help protect you from some difficult feelings; dialogue with it.

Each subpersonality is like a loyal soldier fighting a battle for you. However, the war that he is fighting has long been over. He has great intentions but is unconsciously lost in the past. You—as conscious awareness—may need to educate him and bring him into the reality of the present time.

The work is to become aware of, and to love, all parts of yourself. Those parts that seem to be problematic are ones that are calling for awareness and love. Pay attention to your dreams when doing this work because dialogue and shadow work may precipitate dreams that can be very revealing.

Dream Work

Sigmund Freud referred to dreams as the "royal road to the unconscious." They can be a powerful resource when doing shadow work, if we know how to work with them. Dreams are often dismissed because they are nonsensical. We are deeply conditioned to dismiss anything nonrational as having no meaning or little value. But dreams are not intended to make sense, so don't expect them to. Don't try to understand the dream with the logic of the rational mind. Always approach the dream with an open mind. Assume that it has something to teach you.

A dream can be understood only within the context of the dreamer's life. Ask yourself, What was happening in my life at the time of this dream? Dreams are usually precipitated by the events of the day or by the circumstances of your life.

A dream always tells us something that we don't know; it attempts to show us something that we are not seeing. Dreams arise to compensate for the limitations of our conscious awareness. Dreams balance our psychic energy; individuals repeatedly deprived of dreaming become disoriented and often ill.

The initial setting of a dream usually informs us of the general subject of the dream. If we dream that we are in our work environment, then the dream is probably about your relationship with your work or people you work with. If you dream that you are in the kitchen, the dream is likely about your diet or eating habits.

If the dream setting is from your present life circumstances, the dream may be telling you about something that's occurring now in your life. If the dream setting is from your past, then the dream is likely about something in your psyche that formed in the past; but even so, it has some relevance to your present life circumstance, otherwise the dream would not have occurred.

Remember that dreams most often convey subjective information. If you dream about a person, the dream is likely revealing something about your attitude or your relationship with that person, rather than what is objectively true about him or her. But there are times when dreams do inform us about our objective world, so do not summarily dismiss that possibility when you work with a dream.

In dream work, we can use processes similar to those described for working with the shadow and with subpersonalities. You can develop a dialogue with some of the characters in your dream. Let yourself temporarily *become* the various characters in the dream; see what feelings or memories arise. For example, if you dreamt that you were being chased by a monster, then first become yourself in the dream; let yourself feel the fear and whatever else arises. Then become the monster itself, and see what feelings and mental associations may arise. Relive the dream consciously and see what that feels like.

I advise students to be very cautious of using dream dictionaries or any "canned description" of what something means. These can sometimes be helpful, but remember that the meaning of anything in your dream is what it means to you. Take time to develop that meaning. Record all of your internal associations with a particular dream figure and notice your feelings as you do so.

Sometimes it is helpful to look at life itself as a dream. When you experience something that feels meaningful, consider working with that experience as if you just dreamed it. This can provide some very interesting insights!

The Shadow Body

The shadow is reflected in the body. What the mind forgets, the body remembers. Many of our physical ailments—especially chronic ones—may be related to the shadow. In a very real sense, the body is like a museum that displays our personal history; it is like a book that contains the unread biography of our life or a family album that holds the image of our ancestors. Our bodies are comprised of stardust; the history of the universe is contained within each of us.

The mind and the body cannot legitimately be separated. Any perceived separation is simply a product of our own thinking. Every activity of mind—every thought, emotion and desire—registers in the body. If we resist any part of the mind, that resistance is recorded in the body. Resistance translates into tension, rigidity and energy blockage in the body. Resistance in the body blocks the flow of life energy. When our life energy is chronically blocked, dysfunction and disease will result. When we reclaim the shadow, we improve the quality of our physical health.

Thoughts, emotions and desires are energy. Repressed thoughts, emotions and desires are blocked energy. All energy seeks to be expressed; therefore blocked energy creates pressure that can manifest as tension, distress and pain. This blocked energy seeks to express itself when it is activated. This expression can be very painful and sometimes very violent.

The shadow is not just an abstract hypothetical entity; it is comprised of powerful energies that deeply impact the life of the body. The practice of body awareness is very important in shadow work. It can be helpful to engage some body therapies; bodywork can identify and release unconscious patterns of energy blockage. Massage, Rolfing, hatha yoga, tai chi and qigong are examples of some types of bodywork available; there are many other forms.

Most important of all is to love the body. To love the body, we must become deeply aware of it and accept it just as it is. To accept the body as it is does not rule out an attempt to improve the health or the functioning of the body, but if we do so, we always begin by loving the body just as it is. Our acceptance of the body is not conditional upon its appearance or ability to function in a certain way.

We have a great deal of cultural conditioning that's related to body image and functioning that can contribute to shame or hatred of our body. It is very important to discover our present attitude toward our body and then to work with, and release, any judgment that we may be holding toward it.

To love someone is to pay attention to them and to listen to them. A big step in loving the body is learning to listen to it. The body does not speak in the language of the conscious mind; it speaks in its own language. The body speaks to us in sensations and in symptoms. It speaks to us in dreams and in desires. Dialoguing with the body can be very helpful. Have a two-way conversation with your body. Record the dialogue in your journal. When we listen to our body, as it speaks to us, we are honoring it and helping it to heal as well.

Forgiveness

Shadow work is essentially a process of forgiveness. Forgiveness is releasing all blame and condemnation directed toward our self, another person or any group of persons. It means letting go of the belief that anyone is bad, evil or wrong. Forgiveness means taking responsibility for our own response to whatever has occurred.

Authentic forgiveness does not mean suppressing our emotions or memories. It does not mean pretending that nothing ever happened. Forgiveness does not mean that we will not hold another accountable for their actions; but when we do so, it is not with an attitude of vindictiveness.

Forgiveness is both a choice and a process. Suppose, for example, that in the past we have been mistreated by another person. It is natural that we feel anger about what was done to us. But we have a choice as to how we experience that anger. We can direct it into blame, judgment and vengefulness, or we can experience it responsibly, in a way that leads to healing and to freedom. If we stay in blame and nonforgiveness, then the healing process will be arrested. If we choose to authentically forgive, we will move in the direction of healing.

If we choose to authentically forgive, we begin by taking responsibility for our own response to what occurred, simply feeling our feelings without judgment and staying open to what these feelings may be telling us. Anger can be our teacher if we are able to listen to it and express it nonviolently. Used wisely, anger can help us discover our deepest needs and desires and can provide the energy for meeting these needs in responsible and effective ways. The feeling of anger does not have to lead to violence or broken relationships.

Human beings sometimes behave badly; we may cause harm and suffering to others. Bad behavior does not necessarily mean the perpetrator is a bad person. Perpetrators of bad behavior are typically wounded individuals who lack the internal resources and skills to deal with their own pain. To see someone as wounded and unskillful is to see them needing education and healing. To see someone as bad infers they deserve punishment—which is itself a form of violence.

The moral character of the other person is not the central issue; forgiveness is about our self. Forgiveness is a choice to not engage in blame, condemnation or criticism, and instead to engage in the process of healing; it is the choice to work on oneself.

Any form of condemnation toward our self or another is a defense against facing our authentic feelings; it is an attempt to ignore our inner pain by focusing outward, toward another. When we choose to not engage in blame and condemnation, we engage the second phase of forgiveness: The process of healing our own internal wounds. We then proceed with our healing. Forgiveness becomes the healing process itself.

This process includes self-forgiveness. Some find it easier to forgive others than to forgive oneself. But the forgiveness process itself is the same, whether working with yourself or another.

Forgiveness begins as a choice to engage in the process of healing. This may take some time to unfold; thus forgiveness becomes an ongoing process. Jesus was asked how many times we must forgive someone; as many as seven times? He responded, "Not seven, but seventy times seven" (Mt. 18:22), which essentially means forgiveness without limitation.

Forgiveness must become a continuous process, a way of life. We may find ourselves reverting to condemnation and blaming at times. If so, we simply forgive again. The process occurs in cycles, like the process of grieving.

Grief Work

Virtually all of our psychological wounds involve some form of loss: the loss of a relationship; the loss of innocence; the loss of dignity; the loss of a dream; the loss of some part of our self. Shadow work and forgiveness nearly always involve some element of grieving.

Grief is a natural human emotion, but we have been conditioned to grieve—or not—in a particular way. This conditioning came from our family, our peers and our culture. It is important to understand our personal history and our conditioning associated with this emotion.

Children grieve naturally. Little children don't need to be taught how to cry; but they are often taught *not* to cry. In myriad ways, children can be taught that it is not okay to feel and express their feelings of grief. Through role modeling, ridicule or rejection, adults can teach children to suppress their grief. As adults, many of us need to overcome this conditioning and learn how to grieve once again.

Grief is the psyche's natural response to a (perceived) loss. Grief is part of a natural healing process. It occurs in stages, but the stages are iterative—they usually recur, often many times. Exactly how grief is expressed varies greatly from person to person and from culture to culture. Each of us has our own style of grieving.

The specific stages of grief may be portrayed differently by various authors, but most models are fairly similar. The first stage is typically that of shock or denial. In this stage the psyche is saying, "I am not ready to feel this pain right now." This parallels the physiological phenomenon of the body initially not registering pain even though it may be seriously injured. This is likely part of evolution's survival instinct; the body's fight-flight response temporarily overrides the experience of debilitating pain. This is healthy if it is not unduly prolonged.

Eventually denial wears off and next comes anger, sometimes guilt or remorse. In the first stage, we deny awareness of the loss itself. In this stage we recognize the loss, but we do not yet feel the full impact of it. Anger is resistance to fully accepting the loss.

This can be a crucial stage in the process. When someone is stuck in the grief process, it is often at this stage. Because of our social or religious conditioning, some of us do not acknowledge anger. We may see anger as unnecessary or "unspiritual." Denial of anger will stall the healing process.

At times of great loss, it is not unusual to feel angry at God. Some may have difficulty acknowledging this fact. But if it is present, let yourself see it and feel it. Working with someone having this experience, I sometimes say, "Only the most insecure God would be offended by your anger; any God worth believing in will surely understand!"

We can become stuck in projecting anger outward, or inward in the form of blame or guilt. Some may develop a "victim identity" and support this identity by "telling their story" to others. To be certain, some of us have had terrible things happen to us; and we may *have been* a victim at the time of occurrence. Telling our story can be part of the healing process; it is a way of breaking through denial. But sooner or later, if healing is to occur, we must let go of our identification with the story and move onto the next stage of the healing process.

In the third stage, we begin to feel the full impact of our loss. Here is where we feel the deep sadness and emptiness that arise from the loss. This stage is typically the longest and the most challenging. Most defensiveness and resistance are an attempt to avoid this feeling. Grief is sometimes called the "healing feeling." We heal through our mourning. Grieving eventually restores us to wholeness. The following is advice for anyone experiencing grief:

- Live one day at a time. Be as present as you can be to this moment's experience. The future always unfolds from the present moment.

- Have a daily routine that includes both activity and time for doing nothing at all. Have some structure in your life—but not too much.

- Take care of yourself physically; appropriate rest, nutrition and exercise are very important. It is easy to ignore this when in deep grief.

- Make as few critical decisions as possible. Minimize stress as much as you can.

- Develop a healthy support system and rely upon it as needed.

- Pray. Meditate. Nurture your soul. Be gentle with yourself.

When someone is in grief, I may ask them to read Psalm 23, and then remind them of a few things that it tells us:

- At times we must walk through the Valley of the Shadow of Death; we cannot run through it or fly over it. There are no shortcuts or bypasses.

- And yet, it does not tell us to pitch a tent or build a house in the valley. We walk through the valley; it is a journey.

- We walk through the valley one step at a time, one day at a time. The Lord does not carry us through the valley. We have to walk on our own two feet, but we never walk alone. The

Lord—our own true nature—is always present, guiding and protecting us.

Eventually we recover and reap the blessing that was well-disguised by the loss. It may seem like a cliché when we hear that "Every loss is a spiritual gain," but it is absolutely true. What we gain is greater access to own essential nature, the pearl beyond price. I have often shared with others this quote from Alla Bozarth-Campbell:

> Finding my way back to the missing part of myself, reclaiming it from the person or thing now gone, is the process I have called grieving. It is … not only the way we survive hurtful loss, but it is the way we can learn to live more creatively through and beyond the loss, into and out of a deeper part of ourselves.[39]

Developing a Support System

When we are engaged in shadow work and when we are grieving, it is very helpful to have a support system. A reliable support system helps us to continue on the path of healing when we feel lost or overwhelmed. It can give us the encouragement we need when our own faith falters. A support system can know the truth for us when we forget. Friends and relatives may be helpful, but all too often their agenda is to bring us back to our old life—to the person that is familiar to them. Their intentions may be good, but this can prove to be counterproductive for us in the long run.

If possible, find a support system consisting of persons who can support you just as you are—whatever that may be. Counseling or psychotherapy may be called for. Engaging in psychotherapy does not mean that you are sick or broken. This activity may be a wise way to love and support yourself during these times. There is something therapeutic about being fully heard by another human being in a compassionate, nonjudgmental way. This soul-level validation by another person is perhaps the most powerful antidote to the shame that often arises in doing shadow work. We cannot completely heal if we feel isolated. This sense of isolation denies the fundamental truth that we are intrinsically connected to every living being in the universe. Realizing this truth is the key to healing ourselves.

Trusting the Process

Internal support is even more important than external support. Just as drugs and antibiotics may be effective in temporarily healing the body, they cannot be a substitute for our own immune system. So also an external support system cannot be a substitute for our own internal healing system. The most powerful internal support possible is our own essential nature; this is our "psychic immune system."

Yet, as we have seen, in the formation of the false self, we have become unconsciously disconnected from our essential nature, our true self. The essential nature is still there, but we are blind to it, blinded by the trance of the ego identity.

A huge part of our healing comes in the form of learning to trust essential nature once again. Much of our wounding comes in the form of betrayal, and betrayal destroys our ability to trust. As we regain this ability we learn to trust at an even deeper level than before. But this trust is not in another person, nor is it in some god in the sky. Our trust is in life itself. And our trust is in our self—not in the personality, but in our own essential nature, our true self.

In learning to trust, we relax into the flow of life. We see that in spite of our struggling and stumbling there is an Infinite Intelligence that guides the unfolding of our life. I love this wonderful proverb from the Ojibwa: "Sometimes I go about in pity for myself, and all the while, a great wind carries me across the sky."

One summer afternoon at a retreat in the Great Smoky Mountains, I was sitting in meditation next to a clear mountain stream. I had been pondering the strange circuitous journey upon which life had taken me. My mind could not understand why my life had unfolded as it had; I had no idea where it was going from here. As I watched the flow of the mountain stream through half-opened eyes, the following poem composed itself into my aware-ness:

> The heart is like a river
> Winding though time and space,
> Endlessly yearning for the taste of the sea.
> The mind is like a road;
> Hard and straight,
> Stretching from city to town to village;
> Endlessly connecting this to that.
> The journey of the heart
> Makes little sense to the mind:
> "The shortest distance between two points
>   Is a straight line!
>   Why do you wander so aimlessly,
> Wasting time and energy?"
> The heart replies:
>   "As gravity is to water,
> Gathering it ever
> Into the sea,
> So yearning for the divine,
>   Is to the heart,
> Drawing it ever
> Into the One."
> When the heart surrenders to her yearning,
>   Life becomes a river:

> Flowing with no effort,
> Moving with no design—
> And yet,
>> With absolute certainty, knows
> That it is going home.

Our essential nature is not static, because life itself is not static. Nothing in this universe is static, except perhaps our beliefs, our internal maps. When life brings changes, as it will, it challenges the static, fictitious maps we hold in mind. The maps are not bad; we may need them at times—but we have taken them far too seriously. We have identified with them, and we try to hold onto them. These beliefs are like houses built on sand; the tides of change eventually bring them down.

Embracing Wholeness

As we reclaim the lost parts of self, we transform them back into their original nature. As we let go of pieces of ego identification, we discover the essence of who we truly are. When we let go of that which is not real, our essential nature is waiting for us.

By facing the demons within us, we transform them into angels. Our demons are really nothing but rejected angels. As we face and embrace these lost parts of self, we realize the greatest of all paradoxes: That within our self which seems the most intractable, difficult and despicable can provide the greatest blessing.

Grief can deepen the intuitive understanding of the heart; it brings wisdom and maturity. Grief work will open the heart of compassion like nothing else. It brings us to the foundation of what it means to be human, and it unites us there.

Embracing our deepest fears brings awareness of our innate invulnerability. Who we really are can never be hurt, lost or humiliated. Embracing our greatest fear will lead to a deep sense of trust—trust in oneself and trust in life itself.

Anger, when reclaimed, provides access to parts of self that were not available, until now. The former ego strategies are no longer needed because we are directly aware of our own needs and have gained the power to meet these needs in new and more effective ways.

Reclaiming our repressed sexuality gives us access not only to a healthy expression of sexuality itself, but also to new avenues of creative energy. Human sexuality has its roots in our essential nature; it is the evolutionary response to the divine creative impulse. We now have more direct access to that impulse.

Facing our shame and seeing through its unreality gives us deeper awareness of our own innate value and beauty. We see that there is no part of us that is bad or needs to be hidden. We no longer have to prove our worth or our goodness. We discover our original innocence; we discover the original blessing that we truly are.

These words by Derek Walcott poetically summarize the fruits of our journey:

> The time will come
> When, with elation,
> You will greet yourself arriving
> At your own door, in your own mirror,
> And each will smile at the other's welcome.
>
> And say, sit here, Eat.
> You will love again the stranger who was your-
>   self.
> Give wine. Give bread. Give back your heart
> To itself, to the stranger who has loved you
>
> All your life, whom you ignored
> For another, who knows you by heart.

Take down the love letters from the bookshelf,

The photographs, the desperate notes,
Peel your image from the mirror.
Sit. Feast on your life.[40]

The experience of wholeness is that of being complete in each moment. Each moment is enough. One feels a sense of fullness and satisfaction simply in being. Nothing needs to be done, yet all things are possible. One feels the joy of simply being with oneself. We are complete.

In Summary

1. We always are able to reclaim our "lost" essential nature because the essential nature is never lost, only hidden. To heal is to release illusions that have been held in consciousness. We evolve anytime we become more conscious.

2. We reclaim our essential nature by reclaiming the shadow. The shadow houses the energy of our disguised essential nature. The shadow is a mirror of our own conscious attitude toward it.

3. One way to directly reclaim the shadow is as follows. The first step is to recognize our projections. The next step is to dialogue with the shadow symptom. Then dialogue directly with the projected aspect. The final step is to directly experience the quality that is projected. Consciously feel the sensations and emotions that arise.

4. The unconscious is a conglomerate—a collection of various subpersonalities. The conditions in our life can activate them. A subpersonality is a collection of habituated beliefs, emotions and behaviors formed to meet a specific need in our life.

5. Shadow work involves reclaiming these subpersonalities. Each subpersonality was formed to meet a specific need. Determine what that need is. Educate it through dialogue and bring it into reality of the present time.

6. To work with a dream, approach it with an open mind and assume it has something to teach you. Dreams are precipitated by our life circumstances. Dreams compensate for limitations of conscious awareness.

7. The shadow is reflected in the body. If we resist any part of the mind, this is recorded in the body. Body awareness is very important in shadow work; love your body, listen to it, dialogue with it.

8. Shadow work is forgiveness—releasing all blame and con-demnation. Forgiveness does not mean suppression; it means taking responsibility. It is both a choice and a process.

9. Condemnation avoids facing our feelings. Giving up condem-nation begins healing our wounds. Most wounding involves loss. Shadow work involves grieving.

10. Grief is a natural healing process; it occurs in stages. The first stage is denial. The next stage is some form of anger. The third stage is sadness, when we feel the full impact.

11. Advice for experiencing grief: Live one day at a time; have some structure in your life; take care of yourself; develop a support system; nurture your soul.

12. Healing is learning to trust again. Every loss is a spiritual gain; we gain greater access to our essential nature. Facing our demons transforms them into angels. As we love and reclaim the lost self, we transform it. Wholeness is being complete in each moment.

13. Grief will open the heart of compassion. Fear transformed becomes courage and trust. Anger reclaimed provides the power to meet our own needs. Reclaiming sexuality facilitates healthy sexual expressiveness and accesses creative energies. Facing shame and its unreality opens an awareness of our innate value and beauty.

Segue

Having embraced our wholeness, we enter into a more complete expression of our human nature. But being human is not the final stage of our journey—it is but one phase of the evolutionary process. Evolution is now calling us to transcend human nature itself. For this we need to develop a spiritual practice—one that embraces our humanity and takes us beyond it.

5

Waking Up

The evolution of consciousness is the evolution of self-identity. Each level on the ladder of evolution has a different answer to the question "Who am I?" The experience of *me* changes at each level. And since our experience of reality co-arises with our sense of self, we can also say that our experience of reality changes with each level of evolution.

Consciousness evolves by ascending through a series of levels following this general pattern:

1. Established at a given level, we have a clear sense of self-identity and of our reality.
2. At some point, we become dissatisfied with our existing sense of reality and/or we glimpse a greater reality and feel drawn toward it.
3. Before we transcend to the next level, we must integrate all the aspects of self that have been repressed. So we engage the work of integrating disowned elements of self; we do shadow work.
4. Eventually we become integrated as a congruent self; we experience a sense of wholeness and well-being. But the evolutionary impulse pulls us upward.

5. To transcend to the next level, we need to let go of all that keeps us attached to the existing level. We begin the work of disengagement, nonattachment and complete surrender.
6. Eventually we die to the old sense of self, and we are reborn into a greater reality. We transcend to the next level of evolution.
7. Now established at a higher level, the self-identity continues to evolve, following the general pattern described above.[41]

Imagine a party of mountain climbers who are ascending a great mountain. Some of the climbers are part of a forward group whose task it is to trek upward to new heights. Others are part of a supply group whose task it is to provide supplies and equipment to the forward group. The forward group departs base camp and ascends with their eyes on the summit. But they cannot operate independent of the supply group for very long; they can climb only so far before they must wait for the supply group to catch up. The forward group must temporarily turn their attention away from the summit of the mountain to the supply group below them. In order to transcend to the mountain summit, the forward group must continuously incorporate the supplies from below. This climbing party must integrate all parts of itself to ensure a successful climb.

Transcendence

In the previous chapter we looked at the work of embracing the shadow; this is the process of integration. As we integrate the shadow, we actualize a fuller potential of our human nature. But ultimately we are more than human. Human nature is *not* the end of our journey, only a stage in our evolution. We are spiritual beings now having a human experience. Once again we quote Nikos Kazantzakis: "The human being is a centaur ... his body from breast to head is worked on and tormented by the merciless Cry. He has been fighting ... to draw himself, like a sword, out of his animalistic scabbard. He is also fighting ... to draw himself out of his human scabbard."[42]

We have seen that the Cry has also been called the *élan vital* and *radial energy* and the *evolutionary impulse*. Whatever we call it, it will not leave us alone. It demands that we evolve. In the Great Chain of Being, evolutionary progression is from Matter to Body to Mind to Soul to Spirit. At this point in our journey we have identified primarily with Mind, but many are being called to the next level—the Soul level.

Before we transcend to this level, we must fully integrate Body and Mind. Many today are trying to transcend to the Soul level without first integrating the body and shadow elements of mind. This does not work. We may glimpse the light "above us," but to fully embrace that light, we must first turn around and embrace the shadow "below" (as discussed in Chapter 4).

Paradoxically, the self that seeks to embody the light is *not* the self that will actually do so, because it is unconscious identification with this self that is preventing the transcendence that is consciously desired. In the words of Ken Wilber, "What on the surface we fervently desire, in the depths we successfully prevent."[43] To transcend to the physical and mental levels, we must be willing to let go of the self with which we identify.

The Enigma of Desire

We have reached the point in human development where we must now become conscious of our evolution. We must choose to evolve, or not. The question now before us is "What do truly we want?"

This question has been central to Hinduism for a very long time. Hindu teachings place human desire into four developmental categories. The first desire of humanity, say the Hindus, is pleasure. They say that it is perfectly legitimate to pursue this pleasure. But the time will come, in one lifetime or another, when we discover that pleasure is not enough to provide happiness. The next desire to emerge is that of worldly success: wealth, fame or power. Once again, it is perfectly okay to pursue these goals; once again, in due time, we see that this, too, is not enough.

Eventually we mature to the point where our greatest desire is to be a truly good person and to help others. This is a noble life, indeed, but eventually, even this fails to satisfy our hungry souls. At last, we experience the deepest desire of humanity: liberation (*mukta*). What we all really want is to experience and to express our true nature. Our true nature, says the Hindu, consists of pure being (*sat*), infinite awareness (*chit*), and pure bliss (*ananda*).[44]

Clearly, much and perhaps most of humanity has not consciously reached this level of desire, but the number of those who have seems to be increasing rapidly. Once a critical mass has been reached, a tipping point may occur; a threshold may be crossed, after which the process is greatly speeded up.

If our true desire is to awaken, then we must understand the nature of desire itself. We must clearly see both its power to awaken and its power to deceive. Desire may be the most potent force in the human psyche; it forms the very core of our human self-identity. We are born full of desire, and it rarely ceases until the day we die.

Desire is enigmatic. New Thought author H. Emilie Cady writes: "Desire in the heart is always God tapping at the door of your consciousness."[45] And yet the Buddha is quoted as saying, "Desire is the cause of suffering."[46] How can both be true?

Conventional wisdom tells us that what's important is to desire the right things, and to not desire the wrong things. But this turns out to be much more complicated than it first appears. What seems to be the right thing today turns out to be the wrong thing tomorrow! "Right and wrong" are often circumstantial and subject to change. Today's problems were yesterday's solutions. Today's enemies were yesterday's friends.

More to the point, desire as "God tapping at the door of your consciousness" or as "The cause of suffering" fails to address the *object* of our desire; each speaks only of *desire itself.*

Let's explore each of these seemingly contradictory statements: "God tapping" and "the cause of suffering." In Chapter 1 we said, "You, in essence, are the One, dreaming that she is you as an individualized personality." If this is our premise, then it logically follows that the source of all (human) desire is the One itself, because, ultimately, the One is the source of everything. So from this perspective, desire must be "God tapping." But *all* desire? Human desires can, at times, be quite sordid! It seems rather problematic to attribute these dark impulses to the divine!

Ultimately our deepest desire is to experience the One, which is also our own essential nature. But when our essential nature has been repressed and lost to conscious awareness, it will be projected externally onto something or someone in our world. Like a mirage in the desert, the external appearance can seem very real; and like the thirsty traveler, we may journey a long way only to discover that this mirage cannot satisfy us.

Desire may be likened to pure water from a mountain spring that flows for many miles and gradually becomes polluted with sewage and toxins before it reaches the sea. Desire from the wellspring of the heart is pure, creative and powerful; but filtered through the shadowy unconscious, it can become polluted with greed, lust and hatred before it surfaces. The divine may be at the source of our desires, but our awareness and expression of these desires can become quite polluted with negative human energies!

"Desire is the cause of suffering" is taken from the second of the Four Noble Truths that form the foundation of the teachings of Siddhartha Gautama, who became known as the Buddha. In the Second Noble Truth the word *desire* is translated from the Sanskrit word *tanha*, which literally means "thirst." Tanha refers to desire in the form of craving, that is, desire with attachment to the object of desire. This is desire that fixates on a particular object as the sole source of its fulfillment. It is the *attachment*, not the desire itself, that is problematic. Desire with attachment can also be called *addiction*.

The Fourth Noble Truth, which prescribes an Eightfold Path as the antidote for suffering, includes the prescription of "Right Desire." "Right Desire," in this context, is desire for liberation; it is the fourth desire (*mukta*) identified in Hinduism. But the desire for liberation itself can be a cause of suffering if we are attached to a particular image of how liberation must look or feel. For this reason, the Buddha repeatedly refused to give any definition of what liberation is or is not. When referring to liberation from suffering, the term that he used was *nirvana*, which literally means "extinction"—this simply refers to the dying out of that which creates suffering. He refused to give this term any theological or psychological definition.

Desire is intrinsic in the evolutionary imperative; it is an essential part of the life force itself. In its pure form, not imbued with attachment, it is an important aspect of the creative process. Pure desire is "God tapping at the door of our consciousness." Desire imbued with attachment is "the cause of all suffering."

Nirvana (liberation) refers to freedom from attachment, from craving, but not necessarily freedom from desire itself. Even a liberated person can become hungry! But a liberated person will not be attached to if, when or how that hunger is satisfied.

Desire and Suffering

Now we explore the relationship between attachment and suffering. Later we will see that attachment forms the very foundation of the ego structure itself as well as the foundation for our experience of external reality.

The First Noble Truth is sometimes rendered "Life is suffering." The teachings of the Buddha were passed down orally for several hundred years before they were committed to writing. What we read today is a highly condensed version of his original teaching. It is important to unpack this very dense statement so that we can begin to understand its meaning.

The word *suffering* is translated from the Pali word *dukkha,* which has no direct translation into English.[47] Approximations include "dissatisfaction," "stress," "anxiety" and "frustration." Some authors liken it to what may be called "the human condition," referring to the chronic sense of dissatisfaction or distress that haunts most of humankind. Whatever we call it, we all know what it is, because it is deeply embedded in the human experience.

Dukkha refers not only to the obvious discomfort denoted by "suffering," but it also refers to any human experience that is less than complete satisfaction. Indeed, much of what we might call pleasure or happiness would fit the Buddha's definition of dukkha because it is not complete satisfaction. Moreover, it depends upon conditions that are subject to change.

Another perspective on the First Noble Truth involves humankind's attempt to find satisfaction in the world of time, space and form. This teaching tells us that this world cannot provide the true satisfaction that we all deeply desire and that our attempts to find it here will produce dissatisfaction and suffering.

The statement "Life is dukkha" may be likened to the statement "I am an alcoholic," which can be the first recognition of a long-standing problem, hitherto denied. Although this recognition may be met with deep chagrin upon first acknowledgement, it can be the beginning of one's recovery from addiction.

The First Noble Truth is not a pessimistic statement telling us that we are all doomed to suffer; it is the beginning of the very process by which we can become free from suffering. With any addiction, denial of a problem ensures its continuation while honest recognition of a problem is the beginning of the solution.

The Second Noble Truth reveals the cause of suffering (*tanha*), and the Third Noble Truth informs us that when we eradicate the cause, we will experience freedom from dukkha. The Third Noble Truth also tells us that it is possible to live completely free from suffering. A supremely optimistic statement indeed!

The Buddha identified three facets to the cause of suffering. The first facet is attachment, also referred to as grasping, craving or clinging. The second is *aversion* or *resistance*. Aversion is the attachment to being rid of something. It refers to the tendency in the mind and body to push away, or attempt to escape from, any experience that is unpleasant or painful. The body becomes tense in anticipation of, or in response to, a painful experience. The mind responds to unpleasantness with fear, anger or judgment. Craving refers to the desire to grasp or possess something, and aversion refers to the desire to destroy or to avoid something. Craving and aversion may be seen as the same force expressed in opposite directions.

The third facet of the cause of suffering is referred to as *delusion*. Delusion is when something false is perceived to be true. Delusion perceives the unreal to be real. When we are not aware of the true cause of our suffering (craving and aversion), we will unconsciously project the cause onto our environment. We will believe that someone or something external to us is responsible for our suffering. This is delusion.

At this point it is very important to discern the difference between pain and suffering. Pain and pleasure are consequences of living in a physical body that contains nerve fibers. Pleasure and pain are inevitable for virtually all animals, including human beings. But pain and suffering are not synonymous. Pain is inevitable, but suffering is not.

External circumstances may cause pleasure or pain in the body. Delusion is the mind's tendency to equate pain with suffering and pleasure with happiness. This leads us to believe that the cause of our suffering or happiness is external and beyond our control. Delusion is unconsciously projecting the cause of our suffering onto the external world rather than seeing that suffering is caused by the mind. When we perceive our suffering to have external causation, we then also look externally for relief from our suffering. This is at the core of all addictive behavior.

Pleasure and pain arise in the body; happiness and suffering arise in the mind. Even when we experience pleasure, we can be suffering. If we are attached to the pleasure, then we will suffer when it ends, which it inevitably will. We may even suffer *as* we experience the pleasure, because we know that it must come to an end, and the anticipation itself can cause suffering if we are attached to the pleasure. Suffering amidst pleasure is our cultural norm.

Delusion perpetuates craving and aversion; therefore it perpetuates suffering. Delusion blinds us to the true cause of our suffering by attributing the cause to something external. Much of the time we cannot control our experience of pain or pleasure because these can have external causations, but we do have the ability to control the experience of suffering or happiness because these always have an internal causation.

A word of caution here to assure that this teaching is not misused. The Buddha gave a sermon referred to as "The Simile of the Snake" in which he said that his teaching is like a snake: if we grasp it wrongly it can cause great suffering.[48] So we want to make sure that this teaching to overcome suffering is not used to create more suffering!

The implication that "suffering is a choice" is not to be used as criticism of our self or another. It is not intended to diminish compassion for our self or anyone else who may experience suffering. To use this teaching as the basis for such a judgment is unwise because it fosters more suffering. The propensity to unknowingly create and perpetuate our suffering is inherent in the human condition—it is not a personal mistake or error. In Buddhist teachings this tendency is referred to as "unskillful or unwise," but never in a condemnatory way, because it is endemic within humanity.

An intriguing aspect of this teaching is the implication that our happiness or our suffering does not depend upon the conditions of our life; it depends *only upon how we respond* to the conditions of our life. The content or conditions of our life do not matter nearly as much as our response to these life conditions. This teaching tells us that we can be happy and free from suffering irrespective of any condition in our life. A truly radical teaching indeed!

It is possible to experience unconditional happiness, but only if we see deeply into the cause of our suffering. This leads us to seek a spiritual practice that facilities this deep seeing. But before we engage the topic of spiritual practice, let's explore the relationship between craving, aversion and delusion, and the formation of the ego itself. This investigation will reveal how deeply these causes of suffering are embedded into our very sense of self.

Suffering and the Ego

Earlier we saw that the ego, our derived sense of self, develops from a strategy designed to get what we need and to avoid pain and anxiety. And we saw that the *core emptiness of the ego itself* is a primary cause of its anxiety. One of the ego's favorite tools for avoidance is *repression*—just bury it! So the ego itself rests upon a foundation of repressed pain and anxiety. The ego is constructed from the causes of suffering and the strategies intended to escape suffering. Craving and aversion, which are the cause of suffering, is the glue that holds the ego structure together.

The ego may be our identity, but it is not who we truly are. Our essential nature, our true self, is, was and always will be free of craving, aversion, delusion and suffering. Our true self is an expression of the One. The false self, which most call *me*, lives only in the dream-sleep of Adam—the trance of maya.

The Sleep of Adam

Let's look at the relationship between the ego, suffering and Adam's slumber—the trance of *maya*. One meaning of the Sanskrit word *maya* is "not that." From the Amritbindu Upanishad we read: "That in whom reside all beings and who resides in all beings, who is the giver of grace to all, the Supreme Soul of the universe, the limitless being—I am that."[49]

"I am That" refers to Brahman, the Cosmic Spirit, the only reality. Maya is "not that." Maya is the veil, the illusion of a dualistic universe in which we appear to exist as separate beings in a matrix of time and space. When that is our reality, we are caught in delusion.

As previously mentioned, delusion is one of the causes of suffering. Delusion is when we believe an illusion to be true; it implies the inability to distinguish between what is real and what is not. Delusion is believing maya to be reality.

Maya is insubstantial and impermanent; it cannot provide satisfaction. The Buddha identified three characteristics of maya, the conditioned world. They are *dukkha* (unsatisfying), *annica* (impermanence) and *anatta* (having no inherent self or reality). Whenever we fail to recognize these characteristics and believe that maya *can* satisfy us, or *is* permanent, or *is* real, then we have created the conditions for suffering to arise.

The same attachment that causes suffering gives maya the appearance of reality. As we saw earlier, due to its core emptiness, the ego is eternally fearful and dissatisfied. It turns outward to assuage its fears and to fill its emptiness. It needs the appearance of an external world to validate its own existence and to find the satisfaction that it cannot find within itself. The ego is validated and promised satisfaction only as it perceives the external world to be satisfying, permanent and real. By defining itself vis-à-vis the appearance of a solid, lasting, real world, capable of providing satisfaction, the ego creates the illusion of its own existence and the existence of a "real world" surrounding it. Thus maya appears to be very real, and it's all done with mirrors!

The ego creates the reality of linear time in a similar manner. Inherently dissatisfied and unwilling to face its own unreality in this moment, the ego creates a "past" to validate its existence and a "future" to provide the promise of satisfaction. To the ego, the present moment—in and of itself—is unbearable, so it looks toward a fictitious future for satisfaction and a fictitious past to validate itself. The ego then defines itself in terms of past and future: who it was and who it will be. It is incapable of defining itself in the present moment because *it does not exist in the present moment*. The ego exists only as a promise and a memory; it has no existence in the reality of the present.

Similarly, quantum physics implies that what we experience as the "real world out there" is a construct—a world of our own creation. We create this world by our perceptions and by our attachment to these perceptions; we project these perceptions from within ourselves onto an unformed energy field, and thereby "create" what appears to be "the real world."[50] Physicist Fred Allen Wolfe writes: "According to the tenets of the complementarity principle, there is no reality until that reality is perceived .... The reason for this ... is that no clear dividing line exists between ourselves and the reality we observe to exist outside of ourselves."[51]

What we "objectively" perceive is then imbued with a perceived meaning based upon memories that we hold. If these memories are denied conscious recognition, then we will unconsciously project some meaning onto the person or thing that is seen. The meaning we project is a reflection of the meaning we have given to our repressed memory. If we see someone who unconsciously reminds us of one who caused us great pain in the past, then our response to this person will be a projection in which we will perceive this person as threatening or dangerous. We will believe that our emotional response is accurately reflecting an external reality. This is the phenomenon of projection. It can also be called *delusion*.

For example, let's say that as we walk down the street, we see a big black dog coming toward us. If we were once bitten by a big black dog, how we respond will depend upon our relationship with our memory of that experience. If we remember it and have healed the trauma then we will feel very little fear. If we have not fully recovered from that trauma, our experience will be emotionally charged with some emotion—perhaps fear. We may recognize the cause of our fear as entirely within our self, as the result of an old memory. But if we have repressed that memory and unconsciously still hold the pain of that experience, we may feel intense fear and perceive the dog to be inherently dangerous. We may engage a story about how such animals should be locked up, all the while unaware that our fear, and all the meaning that we are giving to this dog, is about *us*, and not at all about the dog.

Our perceptions and resulting emotions are based upon memories. These memories are often incomplete or inaccurate. Even if they are totally accurate, they are from the past. They are not the reality of the present moment. When we believe that our perceptions and the meaning we give them portray absolute reality, then we are living in maya—an illusory world. The world we perceive, as well as the very sense of self that perceives it, is defined by internal "ghosts" from the past.

Someone may protest: "Yes, some of my subjective perceptions may not be true, but many of my perceptions can be validated by anyone with the ability to see or hear. If it is an illusion, then why are we all seeing, hearing and touching the same thing? Would this not mean that the world we see is real?"

It is this collective agreement that makes maya so powerful: It is a shared illusion. There are many layers in the veil of maya. Some of these veils are unique to particular cultures or subcultures. In fact, culture could be defined as a group of people that share a particular veil of maya. Some of these veils are common to all human beings; we call this the "objective world." We assume the existence of an objective reality which is "real" because all humans see the same thing. It might be more accurate to call this "consensus reality"—that which is considered real only because we have all agreed that it is.

We humans perceive the same apparent reality primarily because we share a common anatomy. The construction of the human eye and brain accounts for our visual perception of "objective reality." We share a common perceptive mechanism that gives us the appearance of a common reality. We usually believe that reality to be implicit in the objects we see, but it is not. For example, we may look at a bright red apple and say, "The apple is red." We conclude that this is a fact—an objective truth in which everyone will agree. But there is no color inherent in anything we see. Color is not intrinsic in any object itself; color is perceived because of the anatomy of the human eye that captures visible light as it is reflected off an object. A creature with a differently constructed eye or brain may not see red at all.

The known electromagnetic spectrum of radiation ranges from gamma rays, with a wavelength of only .003 billionths of a meter, to that of radio waves up to 3000 meters in length. The visible spectrum of light for the human eye is about 300 billionths of a meter in width.[52] From the known spectrum of electromagnetic radiation we carve out a minuscule slice—less than one tenbillionth—of the visible light spectrum, and we experience our reality almost exclusively within that very narrow band.

At a more subtle level, our language patterns deeply structure how we perceive reality. We think in a particular language. The structure of our language structures our thoughts. Our thoughts structure our beliefs. Our beliefs structure our perceptions. Our perceptions structure our experience of reality.

For example, the English language is generally structured as subject-verb-object: someone acts upon something. "John hit the ball." "Joe fed the dog." "I see the light." English is awkward in its portrayal of process; therefore our perceptions are structured around persons, objects and actions rather than processes. We must portray a process in terms of "something doing something." An example of this is when we say:

> "It is raining."
> "Okay, *what* is raining?"
> "Well, the *rain* is raining?"
> "Okay, what is rain?"
> "Well, rain is what falls when it's raining. Rain is
>   really water; but water doesn't become rain
>   until it rains."

Raining is a process. It can be identified by one word; but in order to communicate in English we must fit that word into the structure of the language and artificially say, "It" is raining. We must turn a process into a noun so that it can be communicated. Another example:

> "The river flows."
> "Okay, then show me a river that does not flow."
> "If it didn't flow then it would not be a river!"

Flow is implicit in the word "river." But to communicate, we must turn the process into a thing, a noun, and then make it *do something*. Therefore, in our culture we are not attuned to the nuances of life as process; we are much more attuned to life as "someone doing something." William James writes:

> Out of this sensible aboriginal muchness, atten-
> tion carves out objects, which conception then
> names and identifies forever .... All these
> abstracted "whats" are merely concepts. The
> intellectual life of man consists almost wholly in
> his substitution of a conceptual order for the per-
> ceptual order in which his experience originally
> comes.[53]

Our sense of reality is learned. We learn it from our families,
our schools, our cultures; it is structured by language and by cultural paradigms. We are steeped in a particular perception of reality from the moment we are born (if not before). Our view of reality becomes self-reinforcing. We believe something to be true so
we act on that assumption and sure enough we prove that it is
true! Others will validate this for us as well.

What the air is to the bird, and the ocean is to the fish, the
mind is to the human being. We are so immersed in the mind and
its contents that we do not see it—*it sees for us.* Reality exists, but
it cannot be comprehended by the rational mind nor described by
language. Yet it can be experienced, because reality is our true
nature.

Waking Up Adam

Soon after his enlightenment, the Buddha passed on the road
a man who was struck by the extraordinary radiance and peace-
fulness of the Buddha's presence. The man stopped and asked,

> "My friend, what are you? Are you a god?"
> "No," said the Buddha.
> "Well, then, are you some kind of magician or
>   wizard?"
> Again the Buddha answered, "No."
> "Are you a man?"

"No."

"Well, friend, then what are you?"

The Buddha replied, "I am awake."

The name "Buddha" means "One who is awake." To be awake is to see beyond the clouded perceptions of the ego, to see beyond the veil of maya and to know reality as it is. To be awake is to see beyond the illusion of a separate self. To see through this illusion is to see through all illusion.

It is our sense of a separate self, the ego, that keeps us asleep. Awakening shows us that we are not separated from other beings; it reveals the great paradox that "I am everything" and "I am nothing," simultaneously. The ego will misinterpret both of these statements. It takes "I am everything" to mean "I can have everything" or "I can know everything." And it takes "I am nothing" to mean "I am insignificant." All of which is untrue.

The ego is nothing *simply because it does not exist*; it is but a dream (sometimes a nightmare!). It does not matter one iota if the dream is "I am wonderful" or "I am miserable." It's all a dream. Its illusory nature has nothing to do with the content.

To see that "I am nothing" does not mean that we have ceased to exist, quite the contrary. When we deeply realize "I am nothing," we see our true existence for the first time. That is when "I am everything" (or, I am That) arises in awareness, for there is nothing that is "other." The Tibetan meditation teacher Kalu Rinpoche said: "You live in illusion and the appearance of things. There is a reality. You are that reality. But you do not know it. If you wake up to that reality, you will know that you are nothing, and, being nothing, you are everything. That is all."[54]

The Practice of Mindfulness

How do we cut through the veil of maya and see the "all and nothing" of self? Since evolution is moving in the direction of greater awareness, let us find a spiritual practice that moves us in that direction—a practice that facilitates the evolution of consciousness. One such practice comes under the general name of *mindfulness.* It has been called "the sword that cuts the veil of maya." This "sword" of mindfulness has two "edges." One edge is that of awareness: simple, direct, continuous awareness. The other edge is that of equanimity. *Equanimity* means "equal-mindedness." It means that all experiences, in the body and in the mind, are fully and equally accepted, as they are, without embellishment, analysis or interpretation.

In the West, awareness is usually instrumental. That is, we use awareness for some particular end, such as to solve a problem, to avoid danger, or to find something that is lost. Awareness is typically used as an instrument in service of some particular motive or desired end.

In mindfulness practice, awareness is considered an end in itself. We practice awareness simply to be aware. We practice awareness to be fully present to our experience of reality. We pay attention to everything that we experience.

Every moment we have a variety of internal experiences—thinking, feeling, sensing, judging and so on. We pay close attention to these. Much of the time we are also engaged in some external activity, such as walking, talking, eating, driving and so forth. We pay attention to this as well.

Our awareness is usually filtered through our thoughts, judgments and memory associations. Almost everything we see or hear will conjure up a whole parade of memories, thoughts and judgments. Usually we don't see things as they are so much as we see them as *we are.*

We cultivate *bare attention,* which means being aware of what is experienced, apart from our thoughts and judgments that may arise. We do not add to, or do anything with, that which comes into awareness: seeing is just seeing; hearing is just hearing; thinking is just thinking; feeling is just feeling. Nothing is considered inherently good, bad, right or wrong—it is just *what's here now*. We avoid analysis, interpretation and judgment as much as we can. When these do show up, as soon as possible, we simply notice that this has occurred, without further judgment or comment.

We don't resist the mind or struggle with it. We simply discern what is directly experienced apart from any meaning that we may give to that experience. What I see, hear, feel or think is simply what it is; it is not inherently good, bad, right or wrong. Any such declarations are meanings that I give to my experience; they are not intrinsic with the experience itself.

Mindfulness practice is paying attention to our attention. We are aware that we are aware; we know where our attention is focused: "When I am seeing, I know that I am seeing. When I am hearing, I know that I am hearing. When I am thinking, I know that I am thinking."

Mindfulness means awareness of the background as well as the foreground of awareness. It means being aware of the space between objects of awareness; being aware of sounds and the silence between sounds; being aware of thoughts and the emptiness between thoughts.

A second key element in this practice is *equanimity*. Acceptance of our internal experiences—our thoughts, feelings, sensations and so on. It means allowing each internal experience to arise without clinging to any of it and without resisting any of it. We allow our inner experiences to unfold naturally and spontaneously without grasping or resisting any of it. Equanimity is open-minded, open-hearted acceptance of each internal experience.

We have a deep tendency to resist pain and to cling to pleasure. Practicing equanimity means that we recognize this clinging and resistance, and then let it go, if we can. But we can't always let it go; most of it seems to occur automatically. If we cannot release it, then we accept the resistance or the clinging itself as our present moment experience. We don't judge clinging or resistance to be bad or wrong, but simply our habituated response to life unfolding in this moment. Whatever arises, including judgment and resistance, is met with simple awareness and equanimity. We just notice this without further judgment, and we don't try to analyze its cause.

This practice can be done anywhere, at any time. Our intention is to be as mindful as possible at all times. We do not set a goal of 100 percent mindfulness, because this is unlikely to happen. We do not set a specific goal, but rather we cultivate an intention. Even a little bit of mindfulness begins to wake us up. And, as we hold this intention over a period of time, we will gradually develop ever greater degrees of mindfulness.

We hold the intention to be mindful in every moment. Awareness practice applies to every experience, internal and external. Equanimity applies primarily to our inner world. In our external world, not everything may be acceptable for us. At times we do need to make changes or corrections to our world. Sometimes we need to say "no" to the conditions in our life. We relate to our outer world with wisdom and compassion, with the intention that our actions reduce the amount of suffering in the world. As we interact with our external world, we bring awareness and equanimity to our inner world.

Mindfulness and Suffering

Mindfulness practice has the ability to dissolve craving, aversion and delusion, which are the causes of dukkha or suffering. Mindfulness has the power to dissolve the illusion of the ego, the separate self. It has the potential to dissolve the illusion of maya, the perception that the world of appearance is real.

We dissolve delusion with direct awareness: bare attention. The filter of the conditioned mind creates maya; as we perceive reality directly and unfiltered by the conditioned mind, we dissolve the illusion of maya. We experience William James' "aboriginal muchness" without naming, identifying or reacting; we experience it directly without interpretation.

Equanimity will dissolve craving and aversion. Equanimity means that all experiences—in the body and in the mind—are fully and equally accepted. Complete acceptance of each inner experience will dissolve craving and aversion.

Often craving and aversion arise automatically despite our intention of acceptance. As this happens, we simply notice the craving or aversion, practicing direct awareness—bare attention, adding nothing to what is here. We can then notice the relationship between the craving or aversion and our experience of suffering. When we see this cause-and-effect relationship clearly and deeply, suffering will cease. The direct awareness of how craving and aversion generates suffering is the beginning of its dissolution. Awareness is very powerful, and it is the lack of awareness of how this works that creates and perpetuates suffering.

When we see, clearly and deeply, that suffering is caused by resistance to pain and attachment to pleasure then we gradually become free from the suffering. When we experience the direct connection between attachment, resistance and suffering then we will quite naturally release this cause of our suffering. When we realize that we can experience pain without suffering and that pleasure does not equal happiness, we begin to live life free from attachment to the capricious fortunes of the world.

To reach this clear level of awareness, we need to take time to hone our skill of mindfulness. We can do this through the practice of meditation. We do not limit mindfulness to periods of meditation. We seek to practice it all of the time, but to sharpen our awareness and equanimity we must engage in periods of formal meditation.

An oft-used metaphor is that of a woodsman and his axe. If the woodsman does not take time to sharpen his axe, then he will soon have trouble cutting wood. Cutting wood is the activity of our everyday life. Meditation is sharpening the axe. Through meditation, we sharpen the skill of mindfulness, which is then brought to bear in our everyday life.

One form of mindfulness meditation is known as Insight Meditation. This practice has the traditional name of *vipassana*, which is a Pali word meaning "clear insight into the nature of reality."[55] As we see clearly into the nature of what is, maya and suffering are dissolved.

Insight Meditation

In meditation, we sit quietly for a period of time. During this quiet time, we focus our attention on one small aspect of our experience and cultivate awareness and acceptance of this experience. Traditionally, one begins focusing upon the breath, and then gradually expands awareness to include body sensations, hearing, thinking, and all mental activity—including emotions. We are careful not to become identified with, or lost in, our thoughts. When this does happen, we simply return awareness to the breath for a period of time. Awareness of the breath anchors us to the reality of the present moment.

By focusing on the breath and returning awareness to the breath whenever we get lost in thinking, we begin to break our identification with the thinking mind. Most of the time our awareness is unconsciously embedded in thinking; this keeps us in the trance of maya. As we become aware of thinking and return awareness to the breath we are breaking the trance of the thinking mind.

After a sufficient period of time, when awareness becomes grounded in the present moment, we can then begin to explore sensations in the body. These sensations are felt directly in the body and by the body. Body awareness eventually reveals heretofore repressed sensations and emotions. Some of these may be strong. Continue to stay directly aware of the body and not get lost in memories or the story connected with the emotion. Again and again, we return to the breath, if we get lost in thinking.

As awareness becomes clearer and under conscious control, we can observe thinking itself without being identified with it or lost in the content. We notice that thinking is just thinking; it is not who we are. Thinking is simply an activity of the mind; we do not imbue it with any special reality.

A meditation retreat provides the opportunity to deepen and broaden our mindfulness practice. We deepen it by exploring the changing experiences of the body and mind ever more clearly and precisely. We broaden our practice by seeing that no experience need be outside the realm of mindfulness practice. One typically remains silent for several days, alternating between sitting and walking meditation. Over time we integrate mindfulness practice into all our activities. The day is spent observing experiences in the body and mind as if one were a scientist observing a specimen under a microscope. With this practice, we are both the observer and the observed; we are both the scientist and the specimen!

The practice of insight meditation gradually dissolves the causes of suffering. Bare attention dissolves delusion (which is projecting the cause or cure of suffering onto external conditions) and it discerns the true causes of our suffering. Acceptance, nonresistance and nonattachment dissolve the tendency to cling to or to resist our present moment experience. We begin to see deeply into the cause of our suffering, and seeing that—even briefly—begins to unravel the mechanism that perpetuates suffering. Continued practice helps us to anchor and integrate these insights into our everyday life.

What About Self-Improvement?

Often questions will arise about changing our thoughts or emotions: "If one is habitually engaged in negative thinking or negative emotions, shouldn't we try to change these? Should we really accept all of our experiences? Why not affirm the positive ones and deny the negative?"

First of all, we are talking about accepting only our subjective, internal experiences. It may be necessary to change our behavior or change some external life conditions. It is okay to do so if we are able, and if the result does not harm anyone. Secondly, accepting an internal experience does not mean clinging to it. We accept each experience in the present moment and remain open to the next experience that arises.

As we become aware and accepting of each experience as it arises, we begin to see that some experiences include suffering and some do not. Experiences are termed "negative" because they involve pain or suffering. Bare attention allows us to see the cause of that suffering. We see that it is not the experience itself that creates suffering but rather it is our internal response to the experience that determines whether or not we suffer. With this insight, one quite naturally begins to let go of the cause of the suffering, the craving or resistance. This practice is not designed to make one temporarily feel better; it is designed to dissolve the foundational cause of suffering itself. When suffering is dissolved, so is that which we call "negativity." This will occur naturally without the need to control our subjective experiences or to judge them as "positive" or "negative." These judgments themselves arise from our conditioning and will perpetuate suffering if we take them as absolute truth.

Another frequently asked question is "When should I simply accept what is and when should I try to change my behavior?" First of all, anytime we want to change something, we must accept the fact that it exists before we can change it. We always start by accepting *what is*. Secondly, if our behavior is harmful to anyone—including our self—then we do whatever we can to change it. If we are in a circumstance where someone else's behavior is causing us harm, then we do whatever we can to change that circumstance or to remove our self from it.

Anytime we want to change our behavior or life conditions, it is very important to explore the motivation for wanting to change. Our desire for change may be driven by an attempt to escape suffering. If so, then we must look first at the fundamental cause of suffering: craving, aversion or delusion. If we have not dissolved the primary cause of our suffering (which is internal), then any attempt to escape it solely by external means will simply lead to more suffering. Engaging mindfulness practice does not mean that we never make changes in our behavior or in our external circumstances, but it does mean that we become fully aware of the intention behind our choices as well as being fully aware of the consequences of our actions.

Mindfulness and Shadow Work

Mindfulness practice has been presented after exploring shadow work because mindfulness works at a deeper layer of the psyche. The shadow is largely the result of personal experience. It is formed fundamentally from our unawareness of craving, aversion and delusion. But dukkha (craving, aversion, delusion) does not arise from personal experience. It is part of the universal human condition, fully installed at birth. Mindfulness practice is aimed at dissolving these forces. Insight Meditation teacher Jack Kornfield writes: "Through the profound practice of insight, through nonidentification and compassion, we reach below the very synapses and cells and free ourselves from the grasp of these instinctive forces."[56]

Mindfulness practice need not be delayed until shadow work is completed, but the right understanding of how each works is very important, otherwise they can work at cross-purposes. Shadow work is the process of embracing and transforming the repressed aspects of the psyche. We have up until now refused to consider these to be part of our self, *so we must identify with these rejected parts.* We must recognize them as part of *me*, and this is a psychotherapeutic process.

In contrast, mindfulness practice focuses on nonidentification with that which seems to be me. This nonidentification takes place through the practice of awareness and equanimity in which we simply notice thinking, feeling, hearing and so on—*but none of it is seen as part of me.* There is no specific *me* other than awareness itself. What may have been previously considered to be *me* or *mine*, such as a thought or emotion, is experienced simply as another object of awareness, which arises and then passes away.

We can do shadow work (in psychotherapy) while we are doing mindfulness as a spiritual practice. Mindfulness can support psychotherapy because awareness is an essential part of any therapeutic process. However, it is very important *to see that each practice has a different objective.* Shadow work is the practice of *integration*; mindfulness is the practice of *transcendence*.

In practicing mindfulness, some buried shadow material may arise. This is an element of self that has been disowned and repressed. It is important to embrace and integrate this via shadow work rather than attempt to prematurely transcend it with mindfulness practice. In each practice we will pay attention to, and accept, our present moment experience. But in shadow work the intention is to embrace each experience as part of one's sense of self; *we embrace the self as real.* In mindfulness practice, we do not embrace the self as a real entity. The self is ultimately an illusion. The self that we embrace in the integration phase is "dissolved" in the transcendence phase of evolution. Each of these is an essential part of conscious evolution.

The Nature of Awareness

Most persons in our culture assume that awareness is a product of the mind. It isn't, at least not the human mind. Awareness is usually seen as product of the mind because culturally we are very much identified with the mind. But the mind is a lens, and a filter, for awareness. It is not the source of it.

The conditioned mind may be likened to a filmstrip. The picture projected onto the screen is analogous to the world that we perceive around us. Awareness is the like the light that shines through the filmstrip. If the frame on the filmstrip is nearly opaque then little light will get through, but the light itself is not diminished. The light is not changed by any image on the filmstrip, no matter how ugly or distorted that image may be.

We can work on improving the images on the screen. This may be good to do, even necessary. But even the most beautiful image on the screen is not the light itself. Through mindfulness practice, we can perceive the light behind the images. We can enjoy the images on the screen with full knowledge that they are only images. In fact, we usually enjoy them more because we are not attached to these images looking a particular way. We may prefer that they look a certain way, but we don't suffer when they do not.

The source of awareness is the One. It is the ultimate source of all awareness and desire. To return home to the One, we must look toward the source of awareness rather than becoming preoccupied with the images on the screen. We do this through the practice of meditation.

Coming Home

Ultimately we discover that who we really are is the One discovering itself under the guise of "me." Our desire to awaken is, in reality, the One seeking to discover itself through the experience of "my" life. All human desires are but projected images of this one fundamental desire.

What we are truly looking for can be found only by turning in the direction of that which is looking. Conscious evolution is our movement in that direction. You are the lens of God's microscope through which God examines God. You are an instrument of the divine—a sense organ, as it were, but an evolving sense organ becoming ever more clear and accurate. What we call "awakening" is simply seeing reality clearly, as it is.

The Bodhisattva

As we come home to our essential nature, we finish one journey only to begin another. Before, we thought that we existed as an individual: an entity separated from other entities. But in seeing that "I am That," we see that this is not so. Nothing, and no one, is "other;" there is only one of us. We then live by these words from the poet Hafiz:

> Greet Yourself in your thousand other forms
> As you mount the hidden tide and travel back
> home.[57]

This is the joy of conscious evolution. It is not for the timid, but it is available to us all. For those responding to the evolutionary imperative, the great Cry, it feels mandatory. This is the path to which we are called.

The vow of the bodhisattva (enlightened being) ceases to be foreign to us, for now we feel every cell in our body joining in these words:

> Beings are numberless; I vow to awaken with
> them.
> Delusions are inexhaustible; I vow to end them.
> Dharma gates are boundless; I vow to enter them.
> Buddha's way is unsurpassable; I vow to become
> it.[58]

In Summary

1. The evolution of consciousness is the evolution of our sense of *me*, as well as our sense of *reality*. Consciousness ascends through a series of levels following a pattern of letting go, integrating ... letting go, transcending ... letting go, integrating.

2. As we integrate the shadow, we actualize our potential as humans. But humanity is just a stage in our evolution. To transcend to the next level, we must be willing to let go of our current self-identity.

3. We must understand the nature of desire itself and see its power to awaken and to deceive. Desire is at the core of our identity. Desire is enigmatic.

4. Cady writes: "Desire in the heart is always God tapping at the door of your consciousness." The Buddha teaches: "Desire is the cause of suffering." Our deepest desire is to experience our own essential nature, but when our essence has been repressed, desire will be projected outward. Desire from the heart is pure, but filtered through the mind, it can be polluted.

5. Desire, as "the cause of suffering," refers to *craving*, which is desire with attachment. Attachment is problematic—not desire itself. Pure desire is "God tapping at the door of our consciousness." Desire with attachment is "the cause of suffering."

6. In the Buddha's First Noble Truth, the word *suffering* is translated from *dukkha*, which can be interpreted as "dissatisfaction." Dukkha refers to humankind's attempt to find permanent satisfaction in a world that cannot provide it.

7. The First Noble Truth is the beginning of a process by which we become free from suffering. The Second Noble Truth reveals the cause of suffering, and the Third Noble Truth says that as we eradicate the cause, we experience liberation.

8. The Buddha identified three facets to the cause of dukkha. The first is attachment or craving. The second is aversion or resistance. The third facet is delusion. Delusion is when something false is perceived to be true. Unaware of the true cause of suffering, we project the cause onto our environment; this is delusion.

9. We discern a difference between pain and suffering; they are not synonymous. Pain is inevitable, but suffering is not. Pleasure and pain are of the body; suffering is caused by the mind. Delusion blinds us to the true cause of suffering by attributing our suffering to conditions in our life.

10. Craving and aversion are like glue holding the ego structure together. Maya is the illusion of a dualistic universe where we appear to exist as separate beings. This delusion is a cause (and a result) of suffering.

11. Maya appears to be real only because of our attachment to it. We create our world through our perceptions; we make it seem real by our attachment to these perceptions. Our perceptions are based upon the past. The world and our self are then defined by these "ghosts from the past."

12. It is a collective agreement that makes maya so powerful: it is a shared illusion. Our sense of reality is learned through others.

13. To be awake is to see beyond the illusion of a separate self. It is this ego that keeps us asleep. Awakening shows us that we are not separate.

14. One practice to see through maya is *mindfulness*, which consists of *awareness*—simple, direct, continuous awareness—and *equanimity*, which means that all experiences in body and mind are fully and equally accepted, just as they are.

15. Mindfulness practice is paying attention to our attention: We are aware that we are aware. The intention is to be as mindful as possible, at all times. Awareness practice applies to every

experience—internal and external. Equanimity applies to our inner world; at times we need to make changes to our outer world.

16. Mindfulness practice has the potential to dissolve craving, aversion and delusion, which are the causes of dukkha. It has the potential to dissolve the illusion of ego and of maya.

17. As we see that suffering is caused by resistance to pain and attachment to pleasure, we become free from suffering. To reach this clear level of awareness, we must engage a meditation practice.

18. Mindfulness works deeper than shadow work. Understanding how each of these works is important. Shadow work is the process of identifying with rejected parts of self; we must claim them as part of our self. Mindfulness practice is nonidentification with the self.

19. Shadow work is the practice of integration; mindfulness is the practice of transcendence. The self that we embrace in the integration phase is "dissolved" in the transcendence phase. Each of these is an essential part of conscious evolution.

20. What we are truly looking for can be found only in the direction of that which is looking. Conscious evolution is movement in that direction.

Segue

We have completed our personal journey only to find that we are not a person! "I am That." We are the world—and all that is in it. As such, we have not awakened until all beings are awakened. We see that the vow of the bodhisattva is not that of some self-sacrificing saint; nor is it that of a co-dependent holy person trying to save the world. We have arrived at the place where we see that the vow of the bodhisattva is as natural as a mother caring for her children, because there is only One of us.

6

Birthing a Greater Reality

You are the One dreaming that you are a human being living within time and space. In this dream you were born and you will die, you feel fear, pain and limitation. Of course, you *are* that one that exists in time and space, that was born and will die, that feels fear, pain and limitation. You are *both* the dreamer and the dream. You are the born and the never-born. You are mortal and you are deathless.

Your purpose in this life experience is to deeply know both aspects of your nature and to fully embrace each of them. You are here to experience oneness and separation; infinity and limitation, reality and illusion. You are here as the eyes, the ears, the hands and the feet of the One.

Now you are ready to become *even more* than this. You are ready to become a *co-creator* of the universe. You are no longer merely a creature. As a child of God, you are ready for an unlimited partnership with the divine. You are ready because you have answered the call. You know that you are ready because the very cells of your body are alive with the desire of co-creation. You are no longer simply the product of evolution; you are becoming the producer as well. You have become the evolutionary impulse itself.

Andrew Cohen describes what he calls *an evolutionary:* "When we awaken ... we are no longer living the life of the ego.... We are living for the whole cosmos.... We are carried by what feels like a cosmic momentum, stretching way beyond ourselves towards an as-yet-unmanifest higher potential. Inexplicably, we are drawn to fulfill a glorious promise that seems to be ever calling us to itself."[59] Perhaps this is the 21st-century bodhisattva—the evolutionary bodhisattva. You are invited to become one.

As a "conscious evolutionary" you have stepped into a new dimension of living: You, as you have known yourself, are no longer living your life. The universe is living its life through you. Your body, your mind, your relationships and your life circumstances are but instruments for the cosmos to create new worlds. You are ready to birth a new reality, a greater reality than could be dreamed of by the ego-self.

Jesus of Nazareth was a conscious evolutionary. For Charles Fillmore, "Jesus Christ is the type of a new race now forming on earth. Those who incorporate into consciousness the Christ principles are its members...."[60] Fillmore also states: "There is a great awakening, in all parts of the world, to the absolute necessity and immediate possibility of a race of humans patterned after Jesus of Nazareth. This is germinating the seed of the new race that Jesus sowed."[61]

Conscious evolutionaries have lived before and after the time of Jesus. The time period approximately 800 BCE to 200 CE is referenced as the Axial Age. In this time period, Socrates, Plato, Siddhartha Gautama (The Buddha), Confucius, Zarathustra, Jesus of Nazareth, Muhammad and Lao Tzu were born. Each one of these men had a profound influence upon human thought, lasting to this very day. Each was a founder, or central influence, in a religious or philosophical movement that has shaped the course of world history.

Some have suggested that the period 1650 CE to 1800 CE, now known as the Enlightenment, was a "Second Axial Age."[62] In this period lived many seminal thinkers, artists and mystics whose work deeply influences us today. A partial list includes Godfrey Leibniz, Georg Hegel, William Wordsworth, Ludwig van Beethoven, Wolfgang Amadeus Mozart, Immanuel Kant, Emmanuel Swedenborg, Johann Wolfgang von Goethe, René Descartes, Isaac Newton, William Blake, David Hume, Voltaire, John Locke, Blaise Pascal, Immanuel Kant, Thomas Jefferson and Benjamin Franklin. The French Revolution and the American Revolution—along with the drafting and signing of the Declaration of Independence—occurred in this period.

Perhaps the period 1840 CE to 1900 CE could be called the "New Thought Axial Age." This period encompasses the birth of the New Thought movement; it includes the births of Charles and Myrtle Fillmore, Ernest Holmes, Melinda Cramer, Nona Brooks, and Emma Curtis Hopkins. Each of these was a seminal figure in the New Thought movement.[63] Also living in this period were Ralph Waldo Emerson, Walt Whitman and Henry David Thoreau, each a key figure in the Transcendentalist movement, which had a major impact on New Thought. The pioneers of modern psychology, Sigmund Freud, Carl Jung and William James, were also born in this period.

We stand on the shoulders of giants; we may be the shoulders for future generations—if we act wisely. Like links in a chain, each of us is connected to a past and a future that pulls us in the direction of conscious evolution. Before discussing our connection to this chain, which involves both the deepest desire of the heart and the great cosmic momentum of evolution, I want to survey the wisdom gleaned from some of the giants that we have discussed thus far: Gebser, Teilhard, Graves and Fillmore. We will use their collective wisdom to guide our journey home.

A Quick Survey of the Signposts of Evolution

Evolution proceeds through fits and starts; it is rarely a smooth or even process. Teilhard tells us that evolution does not unfold in a straight line, like an arrow aimed at a target, but instead it proceeds chaotically, like someone groping in the dark. However, this groping is purposeful, directed. Like a grassland fire, it fans out in many directions at varying speeds, but moves most swiftly and relentlessly in the direction in which the wind blows. Thus is the "directed chaos" of evolution. We continue to explore the direction in which Spirit is moving life and consciousness. We study these evolutionary weathervanes because it appears that we have arrived at a crucial point in our history: We are poised at the threshold of a terrifying breakdown, or a tremendous breakthrough, in the evolution of consciousness. Perhaps these outcomes are not mutually exclusive.

Teilhard said that to survive we must evolve into a superior form of existence, which he called *the hyperpersonal*. To do this we have to "walk in the direction of the lines drawn by evolution."[64] To Teilhard this meant that we will survive only if we evolve into a collective human organism, bound together by a center-to-center connection that he called love. In this state, we become as one organism, yet we do not lose our individuality. In fact, we immensely deepen our individuality by virtue of a state of consciousness he termed *hyperreflection*. We will become even more of a unique individual and simultaneously more united as a human community. As we go deeper into our own nature, we discover that we are united with all beings.

Teilhard said that to reach this state of hyperreflection, the ego must constantly abandon itself. He referred to the words of Jesus: "Whoever finds his life will lose it, and whoever loses his life for my sake will find it" (Mt. 10:39). The ego separates us; our essential nature unites us. Through this process of continuous abandonment of the ego and discovery of the essential self, we are being carried toward an ultimate destiny that Teilhard called the *Omega Point*. In the opening chapter, I described a twofold human purpose: to fully experience our individuality—our limited nature—and simultaneously to realize our unlimited nature as an expression of the One. Teilhard would say that this is our purpose and our destiny.

Like Teilhard, the German philosopher Jean Gebser believed that we are at a critical time in human history: We must evolve or possibly perish. He identified five structures of consciousness that he said were animated by the *Ever-Present-Origin*. Each structure has a unique way of experiencing life and interpreting reality. Each structure has a unique perception of space and time. Humanity evolves through these structures in ladder-like fashion.

Gebser defined our present structure of consciousness as *Mental*. This structure has been in place for at least 2,500 years (coinciding with the beginning of the Axial Age.) This structure is characterized by humanity's identification with thought; it includes what we have called *the ego*, as we now experience it. The *Mental* structure fostered the development of science and civilization as we know it. It has allowed us to gain a remarkable control of the external world, but at the price of alienating our self from it, and from each other.

Gebser deeply believed that a new and radically different form of consciousness is asserting itself in the world. This form of consciousness, which he termed *Integral*, has the potential to transform the fabric of civilization from top to bottom.[65] Some of its characteristics are that time is experienced as an eternal present rather than as a movement from past to present to future, and space is experienced not as an empty void filled with solid objects, but as radiant, alive and suffused with the Ever-Present-Origin. Although Gebser did not seem to base his theories upon the work of Eastern mysticism, Integral appears to be very similar to some of the higher states of consciousness described in Hinduism and Buddhism.

Gebser saw that awakening in consciousness coincided with a withdrawal of projections. Each step up the evolutionary ladder means that we are seeing the world less through our projections and more as it truly is. We experience the world clearly and objectively rather than distorted by the projections arising from ego identification. Gebser also referred to the Integral level as *Aperspectival*, which means that we are no longer limited to viewing life from a single perspective, as in the egoic mental stage, but we now see from a multiplicity of viewpoints; we can see through the eyes of others and appreciate all various perspectives.

Although Teilhard and Gebser used different frameworks and different language to describe their vision, it seems they agree as to the direction in which evolution is moving.

Let's now look again at Spiral Dynamics, which is the work pioneered by Clare Graves and continued by Don Beck. Spiral Dynamics uses structures that Graves referred to as *value memes*, which act as organizing principles that are central to the way that we think. Value memes can influence very large numbers of people, often entire cultures. Deep change within a culture involves changing its value memes. Historically, these changes have occurred in response to changing conditions within a culture and its environment.

Spiral Dynamics identifies these memes by color and places them into one of two tiers. The first tier consists of six memes, and the second tier, at present, consists of two memes. (Higher memes are continuously developing.) We evolve through the spiral in step-wise fashion, each meme transcending and including the memes below it.

According to Don Beck, the largest number of people in the world is at Blue. The Blue Meme is organized around the existence of a higher authority that must be obeyed so that order will prevail in our world. In its healthy form it can inhibit the ego-centered violence of the preceding (Red) meme and unite us within a sense of altruism. In its unhealthy expression this meme can foster extreme nationalism and religious fundamentalism.

The dominant meme in the United States today is the Orange Meme, which is organized around the principle of strategic enterprise as a means to achieve success. This is the meme which birthed science, capitalism and democracy. In its healthy expression it optimizes individual development that is not encouraged in the Blue Meme. The healthy form of Orange fosters creativity, freedom and personal initiative. In its unhealthy expression, it fosters materialism, isolation and a lack of care for others or for the environment. Although not the largest meme in terms of world population, it is by far the most influential meme in our world today.

According to Beck, the leading edge of human culture is primarily at the level of Green, which is the last level in the first tier. Green is organized around values of inclusion, caring and sensitivity. Human rights, human values and care for the environment are top priorities. Green has birthed many social movements: child welfare, civil rights, feminism, gay rights and the environmental movement, to name just a few. The unhealthy green—which Beck calls the "mean green meme"—is intolerant of other memes and is imbued with a sense of narcissistic entitlement. Unhealthy Green fails to realize that were it not for the work of those functioning at the preceding memes, Green would not have the opportunity to express its own values.

To evolve, we must move into the second tier (Yellow and Turquoise), which means leaping a chasm much larger than those required to move through the first tier memes. One of the chief characteristics of first tier is that each is identified with its world-view as *the only* valid perspective. As we progress upward, we find greater tolerance for other perspectives, yet always the belief that *our* worldview is the only legitimate viewpoint. Moving into second tier requires abandoning exclusive identification with any perspective as the "absolute best." At Yellow, one is able to see from the perspective of any of the memes and can then adopt that perspective which is the most functional within any given cir-cumstance. Moving into second tier must be preceded by a healthy development and an inclusion of all the lower memes. Once again, we see that integration must precede transcendence.

The structure that Graves and Beck call *second tier* sounds quite similar to the structure that Gebser termed *Integral* and both sound much like Teilhard's description of the *hyperpersonal*. I want to be very careful not to conflate these works and imply that each of them is saying exactly the same thing. This would not be accurate, and it would be an injustice to the great minds which developed these theories. However, we can see the fundamental similarities among them.

The co-founder of Unity, Charles Fillmore, did not have a sys-tematic theory for the evolution of consciousness, but in his writ-ings he parallels the ideas of all our above-mentioned authors. In *Atom-Smashing Power of Mind*, he writes, "The new race that is now being born on this planet will develop the unused resources of the mind ... and will bring to the surface the riches of both the subconscious and the superconscious mind."[66] Fillmore had the vision of a greater reality that he believed would become manifest on earth. He and his wife Myrtle did their part in bringing this vision into manifestation, so we honor them, and each of the great souls we've talked about, as we, in turn, do our part to realize the kingdom of heaven on earth.

All Quadrants, All Levels

I now want to mention one more important voice that has barely been heard directly thus far, though his work deeply impacts any serious discussion of conscious evolution. Ken Wilber has written over two dozen books in the past 35 years, including one titled *A Theory of Everything*, which says something about the scope of his vision! His work defies classification, but the simplest way to describe him might be as a philosopher and a transpersonal theorist whose work is the mapping and integration of the entire breadth and depth of human knowledge and experience.

One of his many contributions is that of a simple framework from which to view the entire spectrum of human knowledge. He calls this AQAL: an acronym for *All Quadrants, All Levels*. This framework is a lens that organizes all human knowledge, experience and awareness. It may be seen as a map for the landscape of our own awareness and a way to comprehend all of our life experiences. (See figure 6.1)

AQAL maps human knowledge into one of four quadrants. These quadrants are formed from two dichotomies. One dichotomy (vertical line) is between knowledge that relates to the internal experiences of the individual (such as psychology) and knowledge relating to the external world (such as anatomy). The second dichotomy (horizontal line) distinguishes knowledge relating to individual experience (such as psychology) and knowledge relating to collectively shared experiences (such as cultural anthropology).

The quadrants are referenced UL to designate Upper Left (individual internal); UR for Upper Right (individual external); LL for Lower Left (collective internal); and LR for Lower Right (collective external). All human knowledge can be categorized into one of the four quadrants (UL, UR, LL, LR) depending upon its interior or exterior nature and its individual or collective nature.

AQAL is relevant to our discussion because evolution occurs in all four quadrants. (See figure 6.2) This system locates all knowledge and experience in one of four quadrants, and within each quadrant, on one of the developmental levels. The evolutionary "ladder" that we have referenced earlier actually exists in each of the four quadrants. While our interest has been primarily in the left-hand side of the chart (internal), the left side cannot exist without the right side (external). Evolution in any quadrant is related to and dependent upon correlates in all the other quadrants. For example, UL evolution of individual consciousness is dependent upon the UR level of evolution of the body. Self-awareness (UL) requires a complex brain (UR). A highly evolved culture (LL) requires a complex social system (LR) to support it.

The quadrants are intrinsically related, but not necessarily as a cause-and-effect relationship. Materialistic science assumes that everything on the left side (internal) is simply a by-product of the right side (external), which it calls "the real world." Metaphysical idealism, New Thought's guiding philosophy, assumes the reverse: that the right side (external) is but an effect of the left side (internal).

The Four Quadrants

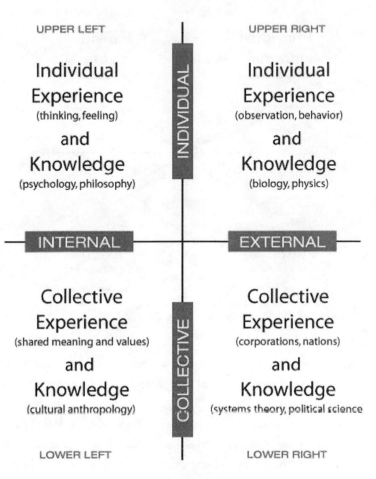

Figure 6.1

Evolution Occurs in All Four Quadrants

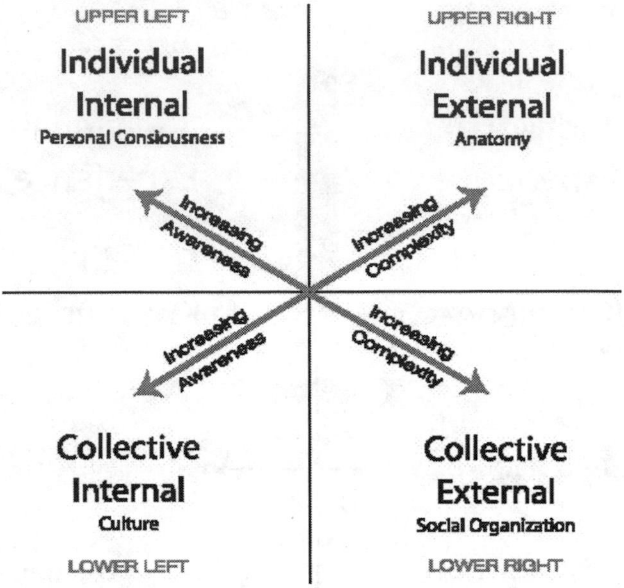

UPPER LEFT	UPPER RIGHT
Individual	**Individual**
Internal	**External**
Personal Consciousness	Anatomy
Collective	**Collective**
Internal	**External**
Culture	Social Organization
LOWER LEFT	LOWER RIGHT

Figure 6.2

We now see that both of these views are partial and incomplete because, in reality, we cannot separate the right from the left. Likewise, we cannot separate the top from the bottom. No individual actually exists in isolation; every individual self is defined vis-à-vis the collective; conversely, the collective is defined by the individuals in the group. These cannot be legitimately separated because all four quadrants exist holistically: they are intrinsically interrelated and interdependent.

We can hypothetically extract one quadrant for study; this is legitimate as long as we acknowledge that we are working within a theoretical framework and not in reality. For example, we can study human anatomy exclusively in the upper-right quadrant; this is how it is usually taught. But to consider the body as a living reality we must also access the upper-left quadrant; we cannot fully understand the human body if we view it only as a lifeless object. To fully understand anything—including evolution—we must consider all four quadrants.[67]

Conscious evolution requires us to be cognizant of the four quadrants. Any project, enterprise or system that we relate to, or study, can best be fully understood using this framework. With AQAL, we can create an integrated vision for any endeavor in which we are engaged. To illustrate, let's say that we are studying a family. To get a complete picture of this family we must study each family member's internal world (such as beliefs, feelings, values) as well as their external world (such as behavior, possessions, hobbies). But we cannot stop there. We must also study the shared experiences within the family; namely the internal world of the family (such as values, beliefs, feelings) and their external world (such as family rituals, activities, communication patterns) as well. To fully understand this family, we need to see how the family members function in all four quadrants.

In our work as conscious evolutionaries, we must see that change in any one quadrant of a system will inevitably affect the three other quadrants. Change can begin in any quadrant, but we must consider the impact in all four quadrants; anytime we fail to consider this, we risk becoming out of balance. Much of the malady of our modern world is due to our ignorance of this. Operating in the egoic consciousness (UL), we seek to fulfill ourselves through external roles and possessions (UR). This has resulted in ecological destruction and an economic system that is grossly out of balance (LR). It also results in a culture focused upon material objects at the expense of psychological and spiritual health (LL). We have become a society of addicts.

The Role of Desire in Conscious Evolution

The deepest desire of everything in this universe, from quarks to quails to quasars, is to return home to the Source. This is our deepest yearning. It is the deepest desire of the heart. But when this desire flows through the filter of the conditioned mind, we can become attached to the objects of our desire. We may become addicted to the world of form. This form may be physical, mental or emotional, but our strongest addiction is to a belief about who we are—this is called *the ego*.

Typically we act on our desires or we suppress them. When we suppress desire, it will reveal itself in shadowy, negative ways. And yet, for obvious reasons, we cannot act on every desire that arises. Still, it may sometimes be wise to act from a desire. Some of our desires may need to be fulfilled externally because this is necessary for our physical well-being. Sometimes we must fulfill a desire so that we can clearly see that this satisfied desire does *not* lead to the eternal bliss that we believed it would. We know that any such bliss is quite temporary and is often followed with considerable suffering. This disillusionment experience is an opportunity to gain important insights into the nature of maya and how we become seduced by it.

One way to skillfully work with desire is to ask, What would be my internal experience if my desire were now fulfilled? Imagine that it is fulfilled and let yourself have that feeling now. Then ask, Now what do I want? Look at what desire arises next, imagine it fulfilled, and experience that feeling. Continue this process asking, What do I really want? Keep going until you have reached the end of all desire. See where it leads you.

Your heart's deepest desire is connecting you to the grand pattern of evolution. There is a divine pattern within your soul speaking to your heart through its deepest desire. Just as DNA patterns govern each cell within our body, so we are as cells in a single body governed by the divine pattern of cosmic evolution. The deepest desire of our heart is exquisitely woven into a larger pattern that balances and fulfills the needs of humanity, the planet and the universe itself. Each of us has a soul-pattern that guides us to the resources and relationships needed to play our part in this grand design.

The Role of Conflict in Conscious Evolution

In the process of involution, Spirit identifies with form to an ever-increasing degree, creating ever-increasing limitation. In the process of evolution, Spirit (disguised as you and me) remembers itself as we awaken to our essential nature. To awaken, we must disidentify (that is, lose or sever the link) with the forms with which we have identified. These forms include the ego, the physical body and the worldview that we have adopted as our reality. To experience the breakthrough of awakening, we must first experience the breakdown of our identification with form.

We saw earlier that humanity's two strongest drives are the drive for self-preservation and the drive for self-transcendence. As consciousness evolves, it threatens the existing sense of self, so the ego identity tends to become more entrenched in self-preservation—and then the struggle begins. This occurs within the individual and collectively within an organization, nation and culture. Represented mythically, it's an epic battle between the forces of good and the forces of evil. We can see this particular myth in stories ranging from the movie *Star Wars* to the Battle of Armageddon described in the Book of Revelation.

Identification with these forms is necessary for our development, but a time comes when the structure and its limitations have served its purpose and must now break down and be released. The eggshell protects and nurtures the embryonic chick. At the appropriate time, it must break down so that the chick can emerge into a new life of greater freedom. If the shell is not broken, the chick will perish. The old forms and identifications may serve us well when we need them, but the time will come for us to emerge into greater freedom and awareness. Perhaps that time is now.

Our personal "shell" may be anything that serves us as a developmental structure: familial relationships, social roles, our identity, our worldview and perhaps our body itself. These structures may be essential to our development, but if we hold on to them too long evolution is arrested and suffering is inevitable. What is real is never lost. We lose only our illusions, but we can become quite attached to them because they seem necessary at times. The pain of breakdown is proportional to our degree of resistance. Breakdowns are not inherently painful. They can even be experienced joyfully if one is awake and nonresistant.

The Role of Religion in Conscious Evolution

One notable area of conflict in our culture involves the topic of religion and religious belief. Let's look at the paradoxical role of religion in the evolution of consciousness. Its impact on human history—for good and for ill—is enormous. Whether we like it or not, religion is not going to go away. It was here before the beginning of recorded history. Humans are inherently religious beings.

In this secular postmodern world, many educated Westerners regard religion with great skepticism. These days we hear much about abuse perpetrated by religious clergy; we hear much about the harm caused by religious fanaticism, and about wars and atrocities committed in the name of religion. Most of this is probably true. But many times throughout human history, religion has also served as a stronghold of values, humanitarianism and human knowledge. Much of the world's wisdom is contained within religious traditions.

It is nearly impossible to distinguish a religion from the culture in which it inhabits. Cultural, and sometimes political, influences are so intertwined with religious organization and practice that we can rarely consider either one separately. Much of the harm perpetrated in the name of religion actually has little to do with religion per se; it has much more to do with politics, economics and cultural bias.

Religion has served to both facilitate and inhibit the evolution of consciousness. Religious movements, like most human endeavors, unfold developmentally. Typically it begins with the spiritual awakening of one person. This person, like most who have awakened, then goes about teaching his or her particular message. The awakened one gathers followers, disciples who are moved by the message. As the movement progresses, an organization begins to evolve. Rules and procedures develop out of a need to maintain the movement.

As long as the leader is alive, he or she usually defines and directs the organization—sometimes obliquely, but always influentially. When the founder dies the teachings are usually formalized. Perhaps a formal creed is adopted. Rituals and structures in the organization may become more rigid. As those who knew the leader firsthand gradually die off, the structure of the organization and its formalized teachings have greater influence. The movement begins to solidify into a religion. In most cases, the founder is glorified—perhaps even deified.

An organization develops an ego identity much as an individual does. The essential nature of the movement, such as the teachings, needs to be perpetuated, so a particular strategy for survival and expansion develops. This strategy eventually becomes the identity of the organization and this identity seeks to protect itself—as all ego structures do. When new ideas arise that seem to challenge the formal creed, they may be resisted, possibly even condemned. (Perhaps even those ideas that would have been embraced by the founder!) A spiritual movement that, at one point in its lifecycle, is a vehicle for evolution, can, at another stage in its lifecycle, be a retardant of evolution.

Today the biggest challenge for religion is to become more relevant in the postmodern world. Many, who may not see religion as pernicious, *do* see it as irrelevant and out of date. Perhaps much of religion *is* irrelevant and out of date. In our study of Spiral Dynamics, we have seen that the Orange Meme emerged about 300 years ago and has been the dominant meme in the West for the past century. The Green Meme first emerged about 150 years ago and has had a significant influence on our culture for the past 50 years. The Blue Meme has been around about 5,000 years and has been dominant much of that time. Religion has been deeply entrenched in the Blue Meme for thousands of years; it has stayed embedded in premodernity (Blue) and it has not changed much to meet the needs of modernity (Orange) or postmodernity (Green). Religion has failed to evolve into the Orange and Green value memes; it has become stuck in its premodern expression and has largely failed to become relevant to our modern and postmodern worlds.

The New Thought movement, which had its genesis about 125 years ago, attempted to bring Christianity into the modern world—into the Orange Meme. It did this with the stated intention of integrating science and religion by creating "Scientific Christianity." Charles Fillmore, co-founder of the Unity movement, writes in *Atom Smashing Power of Mind*: "Jesus understood the deeper things of God's universe …. We are trying to connect his teaching with modern science in order to show the parallel."[68]

The "science" referenced in New Thought is Newtonian science that operates in a largely deterministic paradigm. That is, its principles and formulae are intended to describe what will happen with virtual certainty. Yet since the advent of New Thought, quantum science, chaos and complexity theory have undermined the prevailing paradigm of predictability embedded within Newtonian science. This, plus the deconstructionist tendency of postmodernity, has shifted the prevailing paradigm to that of "uncertainty, filled with qualifications." Undoubtedly this shift has driven many persons into, or deeper into, the presumed certainty of (Blue Meme) religion.

Also impacting religion in the West today is the fact that many Baby Boomers and post-Boomers have become alienated from religion, and perhaps spirituality in any form, due to their childhood experiences with religion, churches and clergy. Many of today's adults have, as children, been subjected to mandatory religious training that was irrelevant, insensitive and often abusive. I have discovered that many persons who call themselves "spiritual, but not religious" still have considerable anger toward Christianity, and perhaps religion in general. Sadly, many of these folks have refused to raise their children in any religious tradition for this very reason.

I believe that religion can, and perhaps must, become a positive force in the evolution of human consciousness. Many people in our culture are starving spiritually. Living in a secular culture, with no spiritual orientation, can leave a deep wound in one's soul. Vast numbers of people today are hungry for spirituality, and are hungry for a sense of community. Both of these needs could be profoundly filled by a religion that is aligned with the forces of conscious evolution.

The New Thought movement is in a position to fill this need. It cannot, and should not, do it alone. There are many other religions, Christian and otherwise, that also have this potential. Conscious evolution is definitely not the province of religion alone; however, New Thought Christianity has the opportunity to make a huge impact on our world now, and for a long time to come. Its teachings must be updated to become more relevant to those at the cutting edge of evolution. The integration of science and spirituality has a very powerful potential, but it needs to be leading-edge science and leading-edge spirituality. In addition, religion needs to become more integrated with psychology. The field of psychology today has advanced far beyond that which was available to the early New Thought teachers; it is a natural adjunct to any relevant religion.

Science, too, has advanced far beyond that which was available to the early New Thought teachers. Fillmore states that he was trying to connect Jesus' teaching with modern science in order to show the parallel. Quantum physics, chaos theory, complexity theory, transpersonal psychology and evolutionary spirituality can be combined with the latest research in biblical archeology and scholarly research in the fields of theology and philosophy to form an extremely powerful force for conscious evolution. With this integration, the teachings of Jesus and other great mystics might be understood in a totally new light. This would continue the work of Myrtle and Charles Fillmore and of other seminal New Thought teachers and carry their work into a whole new paradigm.

Another important mandate for this 21st-century religious movement is to facilitate the healing of those who have been wounded by the unconsciousness of Blue Meme religion and its representatives. To transcend we must first integrate. For many of us this integration would include healing the wounds of an abusive history with religion. This healing process could become a recovery movement similar to the twelve-step programs pioneered by Alcoholics Anonymous over 75 years ago. This could be far-reaching in its impact.

We are not demonizing or vilifying any particular denomination or religious movement; this would not promote healing. For many of us, anger may be an appropriate response because it can be a stage in our healing process, but we must be careful not to get caught up in our blame and criticism. The essential ingredient in any healing process is the recognition and understanding of our wounds and the willingness to engage the process of healing.

Certainly any 21st-century New Thought movement would need to present itself in a format that is relevant to today's culture and today's lifestyle. Perhaps we need new models for ministry. We need not necessarily discard the existing church structure, but we must extend beyond it to find new and creative ways to meet the spiritual needs of humanity at this time in our history.[69]

Guidelines for Conscious Evolutionaries

The pioneers that went before us, those who have been "prototypes of the new race," have left some footprints for us to follow. We, in turn, will leave footprints for others to follow. We are wise to learn from those who have gone before us, and we are wise to know that we must walk our own journey as well. What follows are some teachings that we have gleaned from this work thus far, teachings that are essential to conscious evolutionaries. This is by no means an exhaustive list. I invite you to add your own guidelines to this list as they reveal themselves to you in your journey of conscious evolution.

1. Make friends with paradox.

The nature of existence itself is paradoxical; it appears in many forms. We discussed a core paradox in human nature itself: our drive for self-preservation and our drive for self-transcendence. This dichotomy appears in many ways within the psyche: the desire to bond with another and the desire for autonomy; the desire for freedom and the desire for security; the desire to be known and the desire to remain anonymous.

Any paradox exists only from the perspective of the human mind—it does not exist in reality. The human mind can function only within the context of duality. We know relationship only as subject-object: me and other. The mind must divide, compare and classify in order to understand anything as me or other. This is necessary for us to function at our present stage of evolution, but we must remember that our understanding of reality is simply a product of our present level of evolution. When we attempt to apply our mental processes to ultimate reality, we will always encounter paradox because we are trying to divide the indivisible, limit the unlimited, describe the indescribable.

We began this book with a paradoxical statement of our purpose for being alive: We are here to experience our limited and unlimited nature simultaneously. We are alive to experience the fullness of our humanity and the fullness of our divinity. Who we are contains both of these qualities. This is but one of the many paradoxes of our nature. Nature itself seems to be paradoxical. Matter, at its essence, seems to simultaneously be wave and particle, local and nonlocal, existent and nonexistent.

We encountered the appearance of paradox in our earlier discussions. Spiral Dynamics' notion of second tier memes, which see the legitimacy of each of the first tier memes, is paradoxical to someone in a first tier meme. Each of the first tier memes sees itself as the only legitimate worldview and perceives other memes to be a threat to its legitimacy.

Jean Gebser saw the next stage of our evolution to be the Integral (Aperspectival) structure of consciousness, wherein our worldview contains multiple perspectives simultaneously. It sees time and space as fluid, and matter appears diaphanous because it is transilluminated by the ever-present Origin. This is not comprehensible to the mind at our present level of consciousness.

Spiritual teachers from every age and tradition have baffled us with their paradoxical statements: To find our self, we must lose our self; to live, we must die; yield and overcome; empty and be full. To become everything, we must become nothing. Perhaps this is best summarized by the Indian sage Nisargadatta Maharaj, who said, "Wisdom tells me I am nothing. Love tells me I am everything. And between the two my life flows."[70]

2. Cultivate the power of attention and intention.

Mindfulness practice is a way to liberate oneself from ego identification and the consequent suffering. As discussed previously,
mindfulness can be described as simply "paying attention to
one's attention." With mindfulness we are aware of our awareness. This is sometimes called "being present" or "being awake."

With mindfulness there is no identification with the object of
awareness. For example, when we experience anger, we are typically identified with that anger. (Even if we repress the anger, we
are unconsciously identified with it.) We might say, "I am angry,"
and then engage in a story to justify our anger. We may attempt
to enroll others in our story as a way to further justify our anger.
This is normal, and perhaps understandable. But, whatever the
reason for our anger, we cannot be identified with anger and
happy at the same time. With identification comes suffering.

If we pay attention to anger, noticing the thoughts, the emotions, and the physical sensations that arise, noticing the desire to
retaliate or to enroll others in our story, then something very
interesting will happen: The anger begins to dissipate on its own
accord. Anger, like any negative emotion, feeds upon our identification with it; it feeds upon unconsciousness. With clear and
continued awareness we dissolve the cause of suffering—because
suffering is rooted in unconsciousness.

Attention—which is simply focused awareness—is very powerful and potentially very liberating. It is one of the most effective
tools for conscious evolution. With greater awareness comes
greater freedom of choice; a greater range of options are available
to us. Mindfulness is the key to birthing a greater reality.

A subtle, yet very powerful, object of attention is that of *intention*. Intention is like a compass needle with which we navigate
our journey of life. This may happen consciously or unconsciously, but intention is always at work guiding our way. When
we consciously set an intention, and then practice mindfulness in

our behavior, our speech and our thoughts as a way of staying true to our intention, we will gradually (or perhaps suddenly) see the course of our life following our chosen intention. Eventually we will see our behavior, our speech and our thoughts aligning with our intention with little conscious effort on our part. Intention combined with attention is a powerful system for determining and maintaining our life's direction.

When we align our intention with the direction of evolution, something powerful beyond our understanding is activated. The entire universe will align itself behind our intention, because it is no longer simply ours alone. It is the universe living *its* intention through us. This is what it means to be a *conscious evolutionary.*

3. Embrace everything; be attached to nothing.

Integration precedes transcendence as we ascend the ladder of evolution. The prerequisite for transcendence is integration of our past into the present. We do this by consciously embracing all parts of our self. Embracing all of our self does not mean clinging to, or identifying with, any aspect of self. Embracing each experience means opening to each experience, but not clinging to any particular one.

To embrace another person is to hold them with care and compassion, and then to let them go when it is appropriate. To grasp someone and then never let go is not to embrace them with compassion. It is imprisoning them, and yourself, in some form of a death grip. When we cultivate the intention to embrace all parts of self and all of our experiences, it means that we accept, hold with compassion, and release them at the appropriate time.

In our relationship with others, we seek to embrace everyone with our heart, but with some individuals we may need to physically distance our self from them. Some persons may be harmful to us if we get too close physically or emotionally. We can embrace them in absentia, just as we would embrace a friend or

relative who is deceased—physical proximity is not a require-
ment. What *is* essential is that we hold the intention to skillfully
embrace each experience and each person that appears in our life.

To embrace another person, we may need to first embrace
some part of our self. To embrace someone who has harmed us in
the past, we may first have to embrace the pain that they have
caused. Unforgiveness is a defense against embracing this pain,
but ultimately, we see that the only way to release something is to
embrace it with compassion. Others may create pain in our lives;
no one but ourselves can cause us to suffer.

Nonattachment is not something we can make happen. We
may try to be "detached"—which is an attempt to create an internal distance from our present moment experience. We are
attempting to numb our self against some feeling. We may do this
under the guise of "being spiritual." It isn't. It creates the façade
of "being enlightened," but it's just another masquerade for the
ego.

Nonattachment is not aloofness. It is not "numbing out."
Nonattachment will not occur from egoic willpower. It occurs
only when we are aware of attachment and then embrace it with
mindful compassion. Mindfulness of attachment equals nonattachment. Nonattachment then allows the natural movement of
evolution to carry us to the next stage of our journey.

4. Listen, listen, listen—the universe speaks in a thousand ways.

Our present mental-egoic structure of consciousness shapes
our world far more than most realize. That which we take as reality is simply a construct of the mind. Many in our culture believe
that knowledge comes to us only via the senses; that the only
legitimate source of knowledge is via empirical science and con-
clusions drawn from empiricism. Some in our culture believe that
true knowledge is also given through divine revelation via sacred

scripture. Others believe that legitimate knowledge is also obtainable through intuitive or psychic means. As a culture, we have a very mixed and conflicted epistemology.[71]

Truth can be revealed in an infinite number of ways because truth is what we are. To *be* is to know. Robert Browning writes: "Truth lies within ourselves: it takes no rise from outward things, whatever you may believe."[72] But in egoic identification we separate our sense of self from both being and knowing. We seek truth as if it were outside of us.[73] Only if we feel separated from our essential nature do we seek it outside of ourselves.

Virtually all of us alive today are in the *mental* structure of consciousness as described by Jean Gebser. As such, we see time and space as absolute, we consider the material world as essentially nonliving and devoid of meaning, and perceive ourselves to be embedded in, yet separated from, the world around us. Present-day humanity, deeply embedded in this structure, feels trapped and isolated in a dead and meaningless universe.

In Gebser's *Integral* structure of consciousness, we see the world as alive with meaning and ourselves an intrinsic part of that meaning. We experience a profound sense of belonging and a deep intimacy with the universe. This parallels many accounts of mystical experiences. At the *Integral* stage of consciousness, we know the universe to be endlessly revealing itself to us.

Several years ago I was speaking at a church on the island of Maui. At the church service a young Japanese girl, named Kamiko, played a very beautiful piece of music on the piano. After the service I introduced myself and told her how I appreciated her performance. I did not recognize the composition that she played, so I asked her the name of the composer. With a shy smile, she said "me." She then told me the following story. About three years before (she was 13 at the time) she was with her parents vacationing on Maui. She was swimming alone in shallow water when she noticed three dolphins near her. They were about

30 feet away and were swimming in a circle around her. She was spellbound. They swam in this circle for several minutes and then disappeared.

That night she was awakened by the sound of piano music. Kamiko soon realized that she was the only one who could hear the music. It was coming from inside her. She began to see musical notes in her mind's eye, so she copied these notes on paper. She did so until the music stopped. This scenario continued intermittently for several nights until she had recorded the complete score. The melody that I heard her play was the first one she had recorded. She "composed" several more pieces in this manner. Eventually the phenomenon ceased, but she began to consciously compose music in the conventional way. At age 16 it seemed that she was well on her way to a shining career in musical composition and performance!

I tell this story not to imply that dolphins have supernatural powers, but to illustrate the point that we live in a universe far more intelligent and interconnected than we can imagine. We live in a universe that loves to reveal its nature to us. We just need to be open … and listen.

I meet many people today who are "seeking guidance" about something. This is good as long as we don't become too fixated on how that guidance is to appear. Often I hear it portrayed as some kind of "divine download"—as if the guidance we seek is floating about in cosmic cyberspace! The guidance that we seek is closer than our next breath when we release the mental constructs that create the illusion of separation.

Often the problem is not that we aren't getting the right answers; it's that we are not asking the right questions. Perhaps we need to focus more upon forming the question than getting the answer. I have found much wisdom in these words from the 20th-century German poet Rainer Maria Rilke:

> Have patience with everything that remains
> unsolved in your heart. Try to love the questions
> themselves, like locked rooms and like books
> written in a foreign language. Do not now look
> for the answers. They cannot now be given to
> you because you could not live them. It is a ques-
> tion of experiencing everything. At present you
> need to live the question. Perhaps you will grad-
> ually, without even noticing it, find yourself
> experiencing the answer, some distant day.[74]

Conscious evolution involves asking relevant questions and mindfully living out the answers. The questions we ask are shaped by the intentions that we hold in mind and heart; the answers we receive are forged by the quality of our attention.

5. To birth new worlds, we must dance with chaos.

In Greek mythical cosmogony, Chaos is the original dark void, a divine primordial condition from which everything else appeared. From Chaos emerged Gaia and then Eros. Gaia is a deity in the Greek pantheon known by us as Mother Earth or Mother Nature. Eros is known best as the god of erotic love, but he is also the ever-unfolding creative urge of nature. Eros can be seen as the universal energy of desire.

Conscious evolution sometimes requires that we let go of our existing world in order to birth a new one. When we let go of this world we enter into the realm of Chaos, which is the place where all worlds are born. If we mindfully embrace in chaos, we will birth a new world and new desires. The new desire is that which Andrew Cohen calls *the evolutionary imperative*. It is the universe unfolding its creative urge through our personal life.

Our cultural bias tells us that chaos is bad, that something is wrong. Chaos means that we are out of control, which is not highly valued in our present world. Chaos frightens the ego and shatters the ego's illusion of control. When we realize that this "control" is a complete illusion, then we lose our fear of chaos. With this insight we begin to see that life can be trusted—even chaos, which is an intrinsic part of life itself. To become conscious evolutionaries we must learn to dance with chaos.

Dance partners are both independent and united. They are united by a rhythm to which they are each synchronized. They must be aware of themselves, their partner and the rhythm, all at the same time. To dance with chaos, we must learn its rhythm; we must perceive its hidden patterns.

In recent decades we have been hearing the term *chaos* in a new context, that of mathematics. Chaos theory is a discipline that studies the behavior of certain mathematical systems that are highly sensitive to initial conditions. This sensitivity is popularly referred to as the "butterfly effect." Small differences in initial conditions (such as those due to rounding errors in computation) yield widely diverging outcomes for chaotic systems, rendering long-term prediction impossible. This happens even though these systems are, in theory, deterministic. Being deterministic, these systems are predictable, but this predictability is dependent upon absolute accuracy in measuring the initial conditions. In practice, absolute accuracy is impossible, so the butterfly effect quickly renders the system outcomes as unpredictable.

An example is in weather forecasting, which is possible only up to about a week ahead, despite a theoretical predictability indefinitely into the future. Because weather patterns are chaotic systems, their predictability is highly dependent upon extreme accuracy in recording conditions such as temperature, barometric pressure, wind velocity and so on. Weather prediction is so sensitive to initial conditions that, hypothetically, if we had perfectly accurate measurements from virtually every point on earth, but we missed a butterfly flapping its wings in China, then an unpredicted storm could eventually occur in New York City, rendering our forecast inaccurate.

This principle of the "butterfly effect" tells us that everything we do has an impact; everything we do can make a difference. On December 1, 1955, when Rosa Parks refused to relinquish her seat to a white passenger on a bus in Montgomery, Alabama, she probably had no idea of the course of events that would be set in motion by her personal actions. She would become the "butterfly" triggering historic changes that would continue to unfold until this very day.

Chaos theory shows us that there is hidden order in the universe. As we are willing to dance with chaos in our life (including the chaos in our own mind), we open the door to the possibility of personal and global transformation unfolding in ways we could never predict. The key is to be open and mindful of the hidden rhythms in our life. All things are possible when we learn to dance with this primordial energy.

The Community for Conscious Evolution

Barbara Marx Hubbard writes, "Everything that rises, converges and connects, becomes synergistic and co-creative."[75] According to Teilhard, in order to rise into Omega, we must converge and connect. This convergence, however, is not based upon external factors such as ethnicity or political agreement nor on similarity of belief systems or creeds. We converge and unite based upon "that which is deepest within us all." That which connects us at depth Teilhard called *radial energy*, or more simply, *love*.

As we resonate with the impulse of conscious evolution we find it only natural to bond with others who are "dancing to the same rhythm." Even though we may have few outer similarities, we will find ourselves resonating deeply with other conscious evolutionaries who are united in our soul's purpose.

If you find yourself in resonance with conscious evolution, or experiencing the evolutionary impulse, then I encourage you to reach out to others who share your passion. We bond to evolve; life mandates that we evolve or perish. In bonding with the intention to evolve consciously, we unite so that we may become more than we have been. We surrender our will, not to a group of people, but to our own essential nature. The group then becomes the catalyst for manifesting the fullest potential within each member. It becomes the womb for birthing a greater reality—a reality latent within each of us. Uniting with the intention of birthing a new reality is as old as the universe itself. This is how stars and galaxies are born.

A number of evolutionary communities and networks already exist. You may wish to connect with one of them, or perhaps start your own. If you do, be sure to have a clear intention of your purpose. Vow to live mindfully and to love one another. We are using the term "love" as Teilhard used it: that which unites us center to center. This doesn't mean that we have to always agree or conform at the personality level. In fact, one of the best ways to engage in conscious evolution is to be part of a community where we are challenged by other personalities who share our own deepest purpose. This is great practice for that which we must do as a species: unite at depth in spite of our external differences.

Perhaps these groups and these networks are the seeds for the next stage of our evolution. The importance of such groups can be illustrated by analogy in the world of nature. One of the most fascinating examples of transformation in nature is that of the lowly caterpillar morphing into the majestic butterfly. The freedom and beauty of the butterfly is particularly striking when we consider its very humble origin as a caterpillar.

The body of each caterpillar contains groups of undifferentiated cells called *imaginal discs*. When the caterpillar enters the chrysalis stage, most of its body structure breaks down and dissolves, but the cells in the imaginal discs begin to differentiate and multiply; each imaginal disc eventually develops into an essential part of the butterfly, such as a wing, eye or antenna. These imaginal discs begin their development as the primary structure of the caterpillar disintegrates. They might be likened to Teilhard's description of the peduncle, which may emerge from a phylum that has closed over and appears to be reaching a "dead end."

Perhaps each of us who are experiencing the evolutionary impulse is similar to a cell within an imaginal disc. As the primary body of the existing culture enters a state of decay, we—the cells within each imaginal disc—are beginning to differentiate and to develop. We experience the evolutionary imperative, the call to awaken. Imaginal groups are now emerging in virtually every facet of our society: science, business, education, religion, health care, government, the arts and so forth. Perhaps these "evolutionary imaginal discs" are destined to evolve into the essential structure of the new culture.

As a conscious evolutionary, you are stepping into a new dimension of your life: The universe is now consciously evolving through you. The divine pattern within your soul is being activated through your heart's deepest desire. Pregnant with the potential of a greater reality, you are about to make a quantum leap in fulfilling your purpose in this life, which is to become a fully conscious expression of the One Presence, aka

_____.

(your name here)

In Summary

1. Teilhard said we must evolve into a collective human organism, bonded center to center. By discovering our essential self and abandoning the ego, we move toward this Omega Point.

2. Gebser identified five structures of consciousness. He believed that a radically different form of consciousness is asserting itself in the world: the Integral structure that can transform civilization.

3. Spiral Dynamics uses value memes, which are organizing principles central to the way we think. To evolve we must move into second tier, thereby abandoning our exclusive identification with any one meme. What Graves called *second tier* is similar to Gebser's *Integral* and Teilhard's *hyperpersonal*.

4. To experience awakening, we must experience the breakdown of identification with the forms with which we have identified. Identification with form was necessary for our development, but when the form has served its purpose, it must be released. All we ever really lose is our illusions, but we can be very attached to them!

5. Ken Wilber created a framework from which to view the entire spectrum of human knowledge. He calls this AQAL: an acronym for *All Quadrants, All Levels*. This framework is a lens that organizes all human knowledge, experience and awareness. All human knowledge can be categorized into one of the four quadrants (UL, UR, LL, LR).

6. AQAL is relevant to us because evolution occurs in all four quadrants; within each quadrant there are levels of evolution. The four quadrants exist holistically—they are interrelated and interdependent. To understand evolution, we must consider all four quadrants.

7. That which we desire most is that which desires. Desire is a great paradox: It can imprison or liberate us. When we can allow desire to arise without action or suppression, we open to

the deepest desire of our heart, and this desire is intimately connected with the deepest needs of humanity, the earth and the universe itself.

8. Religion has both facilitated and opposed the evolution of consciousness. A religious movement which, at one point is a vehicle for evolution can, at another stage, be a retardant of evolution. Religion must become relevant in today's world, but it is largely stuck in its premodern expression.

9. New Thought attempted to bring Christianity into the modern world by integrating science and religion. This integration has great potential, but it must be updated into the leading edge of science and religious research.

10. Many people are alienated from religion due to past experiences. Perhaps New Thought can facilitate healing some of these people. New Thought Christianity can become a very powerful force for conscious evolution.

11. We have developed five guidelines for conscious evolutionaries:

Make friends with paradox. The nature of existence itself is paradoxical. These paradoxes exist only in the human mind—not in reality.

Cultivate the power of intention and attention. Attention is one of the most effective tools of conscious evolution. Intention combined with attention is a powerful combination in determining our life direction. When we align our intention with that of evolution, something very powerful is activated.

Embrace everything; be attached to nothing. We integrate our past by embracing all parts of our self. To embrace all of our self means that we accept, hold with compassion, and release at the appropriate time. Nonattachment occurs when we are aware of everything (even our attachments) and embrace it all with compassion.

Listen, listen, listen—the universe speaks in a thousand ways. Truth is what we are. The guidance that we seek is closer than our next breath. Embrace the question and then mindfully live out the answer.

To birth new worlds, we must dance with chaos. All things are possible when we learn to dance with this primordial energy.

12. Join or create a community for conscious evolution. Everything that rises converges, based upon that which is deepest within us all. Be sure to have clear intention of purpose; vow to live mindfully and to love one another—to unite at depth. The universe is now consciously evolving through you.

EPILOGUE

I dreamed that I was walking through a large city. I saw many people of all types; they were all in a rush to get somewhere ... and they seemed to be quite preoccupied. As it was, *I* was not sure where I was going either ... but I, too, seemed to be in a hurry.

Yet at some point an awareness dawned upon me ... "I think this is a dream." But I wasn't sure, so I stopped a man in midstride and said to him, "Is all this real? He looked at me as if I were crazy and said, "Of course it is!" Traveling a bit further into the crowd, I stopped a woman and asked, "Are you real?" The look on her face revealed that she was quite insulted, and then she replied "I am as real as you are!"

As I continued milling through the crowd, I saw an old man with a white beard sitting on a blanket. He seemed to be a *sadhu*—a Hindu holy man. Everyone seemed to ignore him, but I ran up to him and interrupted his meditation by blurting out "Is this all a dream?"

He opened his eyes and looked at me with a knowing smile; then he spoke quietly, "Yes it is … but don't say that too loudly … these people will think that you're crazy."

So the One dreams on … but She begins to awaken…very slowly at first … one person at a time. Yet each awakened person is impelled to awaken others so that an explosion of consciousness occurs … almost imperceptible at first, but very slowly gaining momentum until a veritable tidal wave of awakening emerges, laying the groundwork for a new reality.

We usually begin to awaken by suspecting that we are, in our present state, asleep. We may continue to dream, but it becomes a lucid dream—a dream where the dreamer knows that he or she is dreaming. In some traditions this is a very opportune time for awakening by entering into the dream, interacting with it in a conscious way, and thereby changing not only the dream, but also the dreamer. Through lucid dreaming, we can access parts of self that are hidden and inaccessible to our everyday awareness.

And perhaps, as we gradually live our lives with more lucidity, we serve the One by consciously entering into the realm of apparent ignorance and limitation; a realm inaccessible to a Being that is omniscient and omnipotent. As we awaken from the illusion of ignorance and limitation, we enter that which Jesus called "the kingdom of heaven."

Jesus of Nazareth spent three years teaching about the "kingdom of heaven." He spoke of this kingdom using metaphors and parables. He told us that this kingdom is at hand … and that it is within. He gave us teachings of how we can bring forth this inner kingdom: "When you make the two into one, and when you make the inner like the outer and the outer like the inner, and the upper like the lower, and when you make male and female into a single one … then you will enter the kingdom."[76]

Lost in the dream of separation, we begin to awaken and to enter the kingdom as we see there is no reality in our sense of separation. What appears as opposites is an illusion; in reality there are no boundaries. To awaken is to see the underlying unity of all apparent opposites. The kingdom of heaven is a united kingdom, wherein only unity exists.

Yet we have been dispatched into this dream world of opposites: of separate objects, of clashing desires, of disparate world views. Our work is to bring the kingdom of heaven into the busy city, into the marketplace of human desires, and to live in the serenity of oneness amidst the warring factions of the human mind and heart. In this way, we give birth to a greater reality—a reality based on love and unity, rather than on fear and separation.

Jesus showed us the pathway to this new reality; his only commandment was to "Love one another as I have loved you." He demonstrated this with the life that he lived. Humanity is slowly awakening to the awareness of this transformative power. And perhaps, in the words of Teilhard de Chardin, "The day will come when, after harnessing space, the winds, the tides, gravitation, we shall harness for God the energies of love. And, on that day, for the second time in the history of the world, man will have discovered fire."[77]

PERMISSIONS

Chapter 1: *Oration on the Dignity of Man.* Mary Martin McLaughlin, translator. Used with permission from The Penguin Group (USA) Inc. New York, NY.

Chapter 2: Figures 2.1-2.4. Used with permission from The Phenomenon of Man Project, Inc.

Chapter 4: "Love After Love" from COLLECTED POEMS 1948–1984 by Derek Walcott. Copyright 1986 by Derek Walcott. Reprinted with permission from Farrar, Straus and Giroux, LLC.

Chapter 5: "All the Hemispheres." Translated by Daniel Ladinsky." From the Penguin publication, *The Subject Tonight Is Love: 60 Wild and Sweet Poems of Hafiz,* copyright© by Daniel Ladinsky 1996 and 2003 and used with his permission.

Chapter 6: From the book *Letters to a Young Poet.* Copyright 2000 by Rainer Maria Rilke. Reprinted with permission of New World Library San Rafael, CA. *www.newworldlibrary.com*

ENDNOTES

Chapter 1

[1] Giovanni Pico della Mirandola, "Oration on the Dignity of Man," *The Portable Renaissance Reader*, ed. James Bruce Ross and Mary Martin McLaughlin (New York: Penguin, 1977), 478.

[2] Nikos Kazantzakis, *Report to Greco* (New York: Simon and Schuster, 1961), 278.

[3] Ken Wilber, *Up From Eden: A Transpersonal View of Human Evolution* (Boston: Shambhala, 1981). Wilber refers to this psychological growth as The Atman Project.

[4] John Boodin, quoted in *The Choice Is Always Ours*, ed. Dorothy Berkley Phillips, Elizabeth Boyden Howes and Lucille L. Nixon (New York: Harper and Row, 1975), 35.

Chapter 2

[5] Robert Ornstein, *The Evolution of Consciousness: Of Darwin, Freud, and Cranial Fire: The Origins of the Way We Think* (New York: Simon and Schuster, 1991), 267.

[6] Steve McIntosh, *Integral Consciousness and the Future of Evolution* (St. Paul, MN: Paragon House, 2007), 160.

7 The discourse that follows draws largely on the work of Ken Wilber, especially *Up From Eden* (Boston: Shambala, 1981).

8 Involution does not necessarily occur within time; it is a movement in consciousness. The term *descend* is simply a spatial metaphor and should not be taken literally.

9 Wilber, *Up From Eden*, 308.

10 Allan Combs, *The Radiance of Being: Complexity, Chaos and the Evolution of Consciousness* (St. Paul, MN: Paragon House, 2002), 66-69.

11 Pierre Teilhard de Chardin, *The Phenomenon of Man* (New York: Harper and Row, 1959), 56.

12 Ibid., 265.

13 Ibid., 244. See also *Survival: A Study Guide Based on Teilhard de Chardin's Masterwork "The Phenomenon of Man"* (Northridge, CA: PHENOMENON OF MAN PROJECT INC. 1972), 63-S26, 64-S36, S37.

14 Ibid., 263.

15 Jean Gebser, *The Ever-Present Origin*, tr. Noel Barstad with Algis Mickunas (Athens, OH: Ohio University Press, c1949, 1985), xxvii.

16 James George Frazer, *The Golden Bough* (New York: MacMillan, 1922), 22.

17 Combs, *The Radiance of Being*, 94.

18 Ibid., 98.

19 Ibid., 100-05.

20 Ibid., 102.

21 Gebser, *The Ever-Present Origin*, 297-98.

22 Don Beck, *SDi: Spiral Dynamics in the Integral Age* (Denton, TX: The Spiral Dynamics Group, 2002).

23 Unity: A Path for Spiritual Living, http://av.unityonline.org/en/association/aboutUs/booklet-IdentityWeb.pdf (accessed March 17, 2010).

24 The discourse that follows is original and based on Unity's method of metaphysical interpretation.

Chapter 3

25 The philosopher Aldous Huxley referred to this hidden wisdom tradition in the West as the "Perennial Philosophy," because it behaves like a perennial plant that appears to disappear and die, but then comes back into full blossom after a season.

26 William Wordsworth, "Intimations of Immortality From Recollections of Early Childhood," *Selected Poetry* (New York: Random House, 1950), 541.

27 Jean Houston, *A Mythic Life: Learning to Live Our Greater Story* (New York: Harper Collins, 1996), 65.

28 Quoted in Louann Stahl, *A Most Surprising Song: Exploring the Mystical Experience* (Unity Village, MO: Unity School of Christianity, 1992), 85.

29 Swami Vivekananda, *Vedanta: Voice of Freedom* (St. Louis, MO: Vedanta Society of St Louis, 1986), 59.

30 Wilber, *Up From Eden*, 308.

31 This is what Charles Fillmore called the *adverse ego*: "When the ego attaches itself to sense consciousness." See *The Revealing Word: A Dictionary of Metaphysical Terms* (Lee's Summit, MO: Unity School of Christianity, 1963, c1959), 61.

32 I will use the term *parents* to indicate our primary caregivers, knowing full well that this may not always be the biological parents.

33 C. G. Jung, *Aion: Researches Into the Phenomenology of the Self* (Princeton: Princeton University Press, 1955), 14, 17.

Chapter 4

34 The *complex* exists within the personal unconscious; whereas *archetypes* exist within that which Jung termed the *collective unconscious.*

35 I use the term *caregiver* in the broadest sense of the word to include older siblings, extended family, teachers and other authority figures.

36 For a detailed description of this process, see Ira Progoff, *At a Journal Workshop: Writing to Access the Power of the Unconscious and Evoke Creative Ability* (New York: Penguin/Putnam Books, 1992).

37 For a detailed description of Voice Dialogue, see Hal Stone and Sidra Stone, *Embracing Ourselves: The Voice Dialogue Manual* (Novato, CA: New World Library, 1989).

38 For a more complete study of subpersonalities, see Molly Young Brown, *Unfolding Self: The Practice of Psychosynthesis* (New York: Allworth Press, 2004).

39 Alla Bozarth-Campbell, *Life Is Goodbye/Life Is Hello: Grieving Well Through All Kinds of Loss* (Minneapolis, MN: Compcare Publishers, 1986), 25. Also quoted in Robert Brumet, *Finding Yourself in Transition* (Unity Village, MO: Unity House, 1995), 54.

40 Derek Walcott, "Love After Love," *Collected Poems, 1948-1984* (New York: Farrar, Straus and Giroux, 1986).

Chapter 5

41 This process generally occurs in a sequential fashion; however, the stages may overlap or parallel one another.

42 Ibid.

43 Ken Wilber, *No Boundary: Eastern and Western Approaches to Personal Growth* (Boston: Shambhala, c1979, 2001), 152.

44 Huston Smith, *The Religions of Man* (New York: Harper and Row, c1958, 1965), 72.

45 H. Emilie Cady, *Lessons in Truth: A Course of 12 Lessons in Practical Christianity* (Unity Village, MO: Unity School of Christianity, 1941), 65.

46 Quoted in Huston Smith, 113.

47 *Pali* is an ancient language spoken by Siddhartha Gautama, the Buddha.

48 See *The Middle Length Discourses of the Buddha: A New Translation of the* Majihima Nikaya, tr. Bhikkhu Nanamoli and Bhikkhu Bodhi (Boston: Wisdom Publications, 1995), 224-36. This *nikaya* consists of 152 sermons, of which "The Snake Simile," or "Alagaddupama Sutta," is 22.

49 Quoted in Nisargadatta Maharaj, *I Am That: Talks With Sri Nisargadatta Maharaj*, ed. Sudhakar S. Dikshit, tr. Maurice Frydman (Durham, NC: The Acorn Press, 1990), v.

50 This is according to the Copenhagen interpretation of quantum mechanics, also known as the Bohr Principle of Complementarity, which is the most widely accepted interpretation among physicists.

51 Fred Alan Wolf, *Taking the Quantum Leap: The New Physics for Nonscientists* (New York: Harper and Row, 1981), 128.

52 The visible spectrum of light is the wavelength of approximately 400-700 nm. One nanometer = one billionth of a meter.

53 William James, quoted in Joel Levey and Michelle Levy, *Living in Balance: A Dynamic Approach for Creating Harmony and Wholeness in a Chaotic World* (Berkeley, CA: Conari Press, 1998), 133.

54 Quoted in Joseph Goldstein, *Insight Meditation: The Practice of Freedom* (Boston: Shambhala, c1993, 2003), 113.

55 Vipassana meditation is a common practice of Theravada Buddhism, which is found primarily in Southeastern Asia.

56 Jack Kornfield, *The Wise Heart: A Guide to the Universal Teachings of Buddhist Psychology* (New York: Bantam, 2008), 209. "All the Hemispheres," *The Subject Tonight Is Love: 60 Wild and Sweet Poems of Hafiz*, tr. Daniel Ladinsky (New York: Penguin Group, c1996, 2003).

57 "All the Hemispheres," *The Subject Tonight Is Love: 60 Wild and Sweet Poems of Hafiz*, tr. Daniel Ladinsky (New York: Penguin Group, c1996, 2003).

58 This is one version of the Mahayana vow of the bodhisattva.

Chapter 6

59 Andrewcohen.org, Nov 23 2009 (accessed December 3, 2009).

60 Charles Fillmore, *Atom-Smashing Power of Mind* (Unity Village, MO: Unity Books, c1949, 2003), 33.

61 Ibid., 168.

62 Karen Armstrong, *The Great Transformation: The Beginning of Our Religious Traditions* (New York: Random House, 2006), 356; Bo Strath, http://www.eui.eu/Personal/Strath/Welcome.html?/Personal/Strath/archive/past_conferences/axial-trans.htm (accessed January 17, 2010).

63 Other key New Thought figures living in this period were Phineas Quimby, Warren Felt Evans and Mary Baker Eddy.

64 *Survival: A Study Guide Based on Teilhard de Chardin's Masterwork "The Phenomenon of Man"* (Northridge, CA: PHENOMENON OF MAN PROJECT INC., 1972), 57-T122.

65 Combs, 78.

66 Fillmore, 28.

67 For a more thorough description of AQAL, see Ken Wilber, *A Brief History of Everything* (Boston: Shambala, 1996).

68 Fillmore, 56.

69 This is indeed beginning to happen today. We are seeing many alternative forms of ministry emerge within the New Thought movement. Worship services are taking a variety of new forms and styles. These include TV broadcasts, internet programs and pod casts as well as various types of one-on-one ministry such as counseling, chaplaincy and spiritual direction.

70 Nisargadatta Maharaj, *I Am That*, 269.

71 Epistemology is the philosophy that addresses the question: *How is knowledge acquired?*

72 Robert Browning, "Paracelsus," *Masterpieces of Religious Verse* (New York: Harper and Brothers, 1948), 431.

73 Information may exist outside of us, but true knowledge is always from within.

74 Rainer Maria Rilke, *Letters to a Young Poet*, tr. Joan Burnham (San Rafael, CA: New World Library, 1992), 35.

75 Barbara Marx Hubbard, *Conscious Evolution: Awakening the Power of Our Social Potential* (Novato, CA: New World Library, 1998), 105-06.

Epilogue

76 The Gospel of Thomas, 22b.

77 Pierre Teilhard de Chardin, February 1934, "The Evolution of Chastity," *Toward the Future* (London: Collins, 1975), 86-87.

ABOUT THE AUTHOR

Robert Brumet is the author of *Finding Yourself in Transition*, and *The Quest for Wholeness*, both books published by Unity Books. He has authored many articles for *Unity Magazine* and other Unity publications.

Brumet is an instructor at Unity Institute and Seminary, teaching in the areas of spiritual development, pastoral studies and counseling.

B0038